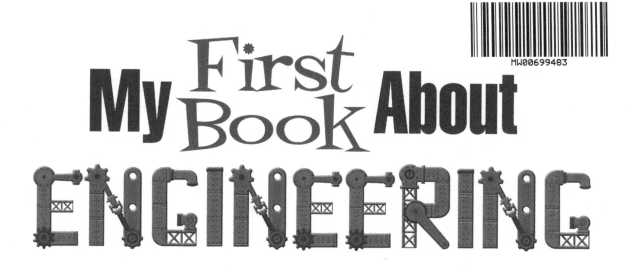

My First Book About ENGINEERING

An Awesome Introduction to Robotics & Other Fields of Engineering

Donald M. Silver
Patricia J. Wynne
Ariel Fleming

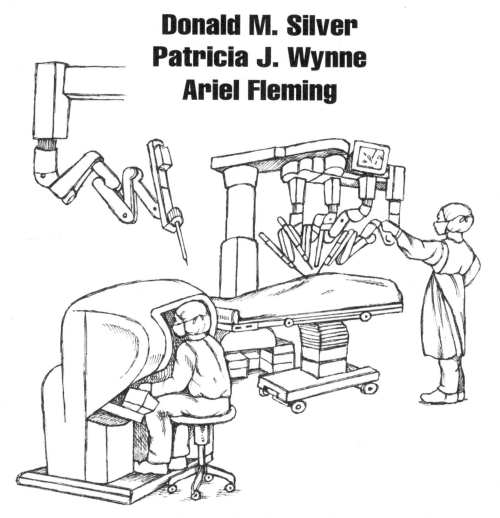

Dover Publications
Garden City, New York

For James Obertis—
So strong, so energetic, so loving and caring for his brother John.
DS

For Joanna Cole—
Whose generosity and creativity inspired children to explore the world of science.

How are robotic arms similar to human arms? What are some of the purposes of the International Space Station? What is binary code, and why is it so important to computers? You'll find out the answers to these and many more questions in this fascinating coloring book! Easy-to-understand captions explain the many types of engineering and their applications to our daily lives. Find out how mathematicians Katherine Johnson and Dorothy Vaughan and mathematician and aerospace engineer Mary Jackson contributed to the US space missions. You'll also learn why structural engineers are so important to the safety of our buildings, and even how biomedical engineers have worked to perfect artificial pacemakers! Plus, you can color each of the amazingly realistic illustrations using colored pencils, crayons, or markers.

Copyright
Copyright © 2021 by Dover Publications
All rights reserved.

Bibliographical Note
My First Book About Engineering: An Awesome Introduction to Robotics & Other Fields of Engineering is a new work, first published by Dover Publications in 2021.

International Standard Book Number
ISBN-13: 978-0-486-84641-5
ISBN-10: 0-486-84641-5

Manufactured in the United States of America
84641501
www.doverpublications.com
2 4 6 8 10 9 7 5 3 1
2021

WELCOME TO ENGINEERING
Engineers design and build things that
don't exist in nature. What kinds of things?
Computers, smartphones, spaceships, and
many of the objects you use every day.

OSCILLOSCOPE
AND VOLTMETER

Engineers use
math and science
to solve problems.

LIDAR
MAPPING

Here is an engineering challenge:
Design a roller coaster that is fun and
exciting to ride.

They also use technology—machines and tools
—to develop new ways of solving problems.

1

ENGINEERING IS SUPERCOOL
Millions of women and men around the world are engineers. They often work in teams designing robots and computers, sending spacecraft to Mars, and helping people in countless ways.

ADD A COUNTRY TO THE TEAM

Engineers get to work with artists and many other professionals on designing the cars, trucks, and planes of tomorrow.

They use math to predict how air will flow around these vehicles of the future.

Graphics and software engineers make the tools artists use to create imaginary worlds in movies and video games.

WHAT IS A ROBOT?
A robot is a machine with a computer "brain" that can be given instructions to do a task to perform on its own. Robots are designed, built, and tested by robotics engineers.

Social robots, like this dog, are fun to play with.

Work robots can be found in many factories. The robots perform their tasks on an assembly line. These giant arm robots build automobiles.

Some robots help fight forest fires. Others help search for survivors after an earthquake.

Swarm robots work together to complete a task.

Some space robots are designed to explore other planets.

3

1 **Learn about cats and other robots**
List what you would like your "catbot" to
be able to do. Gather information about
cats and similar robots that have already
been built and about materials and
equipment that you will need.

TOUCH
A cat uses its
whiskers and its
paws to feel
things.

**SOUND
RECEPTOR**

**SPEAKER
AND MICROPHONE**

**INTERNET
CONNECTION**

Ears tilt to
receive
sounds
better.

SIGHT
Cat eyes adjust their
pupils to let in more
or less light.

— **PUPIL**

**SMELL AND
TASTE**
A cat has many
sensory receptors
for taste and odor.

**ODOR
RECEPTORS**

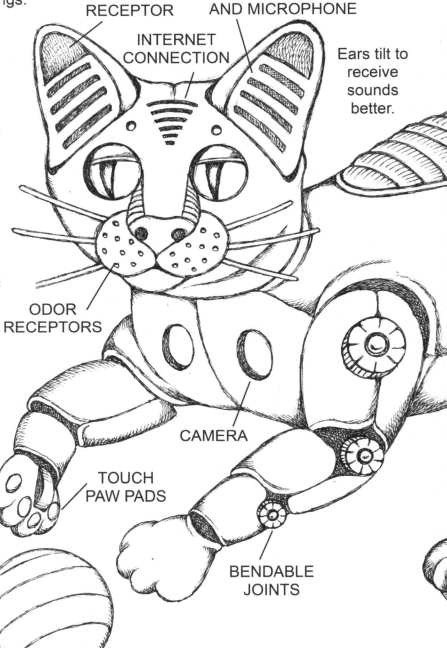

CAMERA

**TOUCH
PAW PADS**

**BENDABLE
JOINTS**

HEARING
Cat's ears are funnels
to collect sound.

4

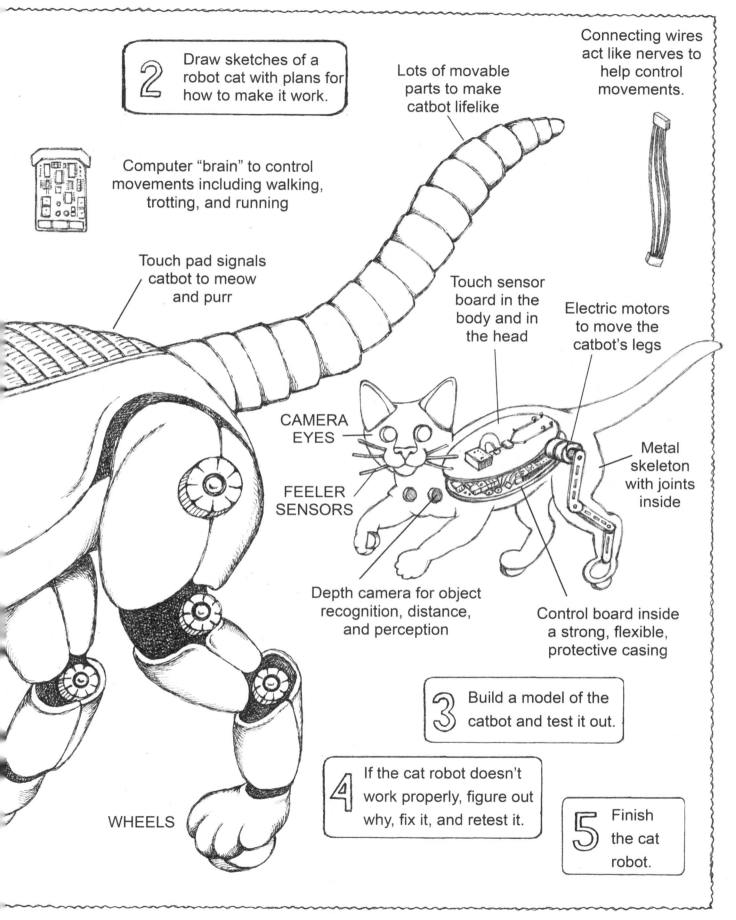

2 Draw sketches of a robot cat with plans for how to make it work.

Lots of movable parts to make catbot lifelike

Connecting wires act like nerves to help control movements.

Computer "brain" to control movements including walking, trotting, and running

Touch pad signals catbot to meow and purr

Touch sensor board in the body and in the head

Electric motors to move the catbot's legs

CAMERA EYES

FEELER SENSORS

Metal skeleton with joints inside

Depth camera for object recognition, distance, and perception

Control board inside a strong, flexible, protective casing

3 Build a model of the catbot and test it out.

4 If the cat robot doesn't work properly, figure out why, fix it, and retest it.

5 Finish the cat robot.

WHEELS

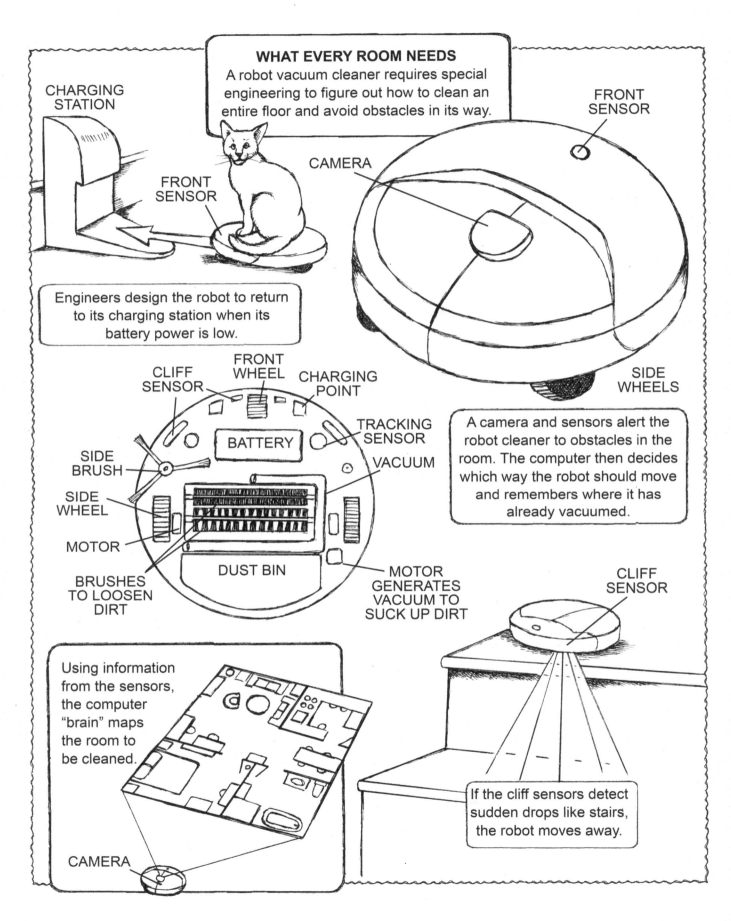

WHAT EVERY ROOM NEEDS
A robot vacuum cleaner requires special engineering to figure out how to clean an entire floor and avoid obstacles in its way.

CHARGING STATION

FRONT SENSOR

FRONT SENSOR

CAMERA

Engineers design the robot to return to its charging station when its battery power is low.

SIDE WHEELS

CLIFF SENSOR

FRONT WHEEL

CHARGING POINT

TRACKING SENSOR

BATTERY

SIDE BRUSH

VACUUM

SIDE WHEEL

MOTOR

BRUSHES TO LOOSEN DIRT

DUST BIN

MOTOR GENERATES VACUUM TO SUCK UP DIRT

A camera and sensors alert the robot cleaner to obstacles in the room. The computer then decides which way the robot should move and remembers where it has already vacuumed.

CLIFF SENSOR

Using information from the sensors, the computer "brain" maps the room to be cleaned.

CAMERA

If the cliff sensors detect sudden drops like stairs, the robot moves away.

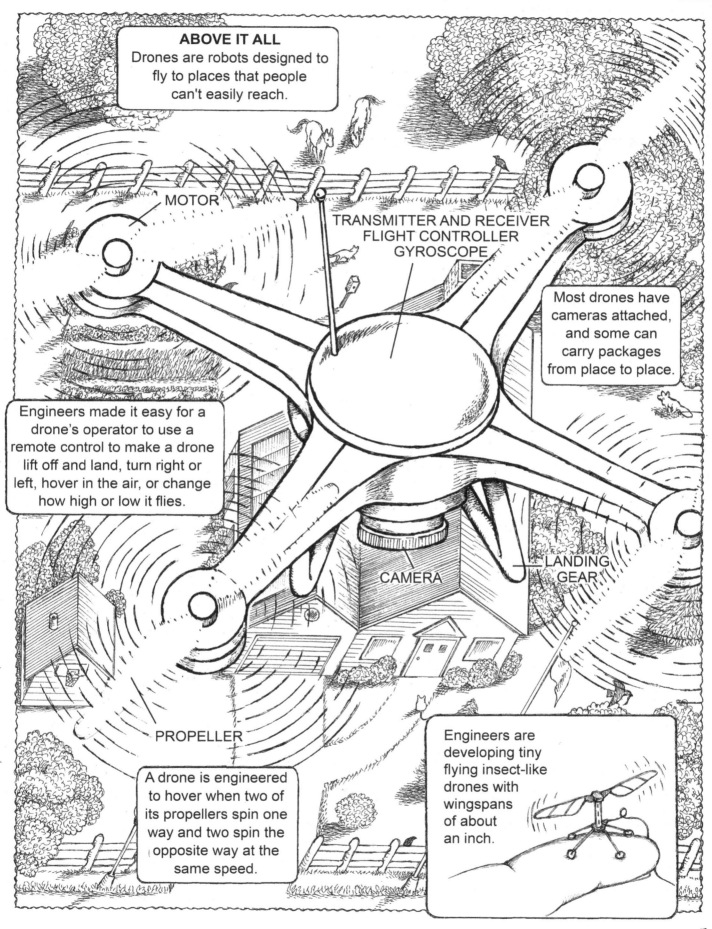

ABOVE IT ALL
Drones are robots designed to fly to places that people can't easily reach.

MOTOR

TRANSMITTER AND RECEIVER
FLIGHT CONTROLLER
GYROSCOPE

Most drones have cameras attached, and some can carry packages from place to place.

Engineers made it easy for a drone's operator to use a remote control to make a drone lift off and land, turn right or left, hover in the air, or change how high or low it flies.

CAMERA

LANDING GEAR

PROPELLER

A drone is engineered to hover when two of its propellers spin one way and two spin the opposite way at the same speed.

Engineers are developing tiny flying insect-like drones with wingspans of about an inch.

7

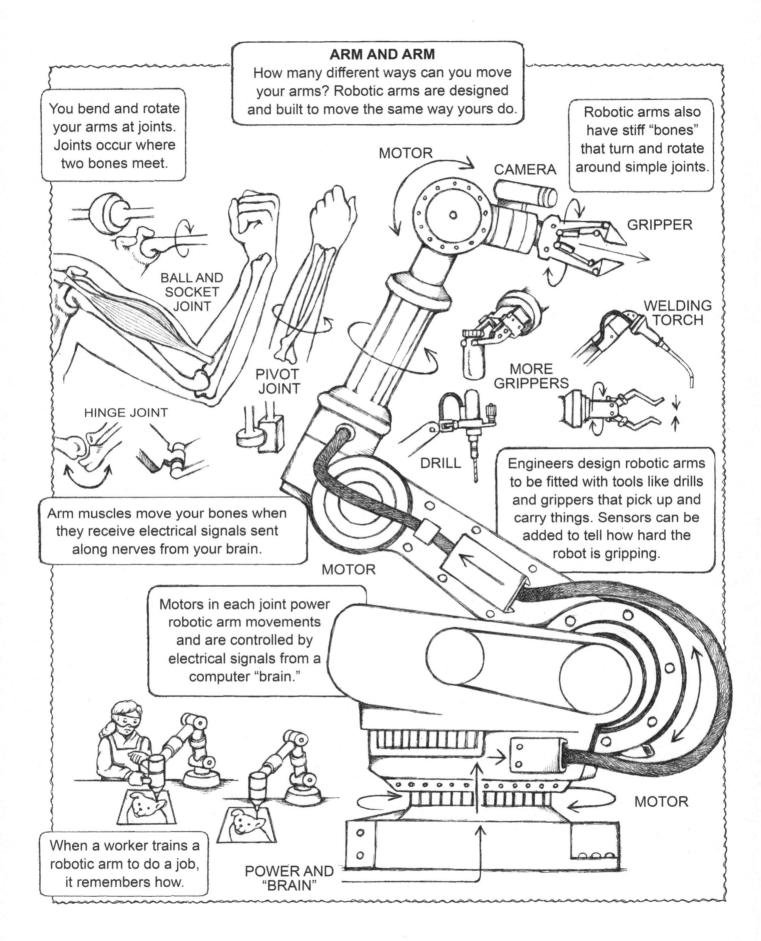

ARM AND ARM
How many different ways can you move your arms? Robotic arms are designed and built to move the same way yours do.

You bend and rotate your arms at joints. Joints occur where two bones meet.

Robotic arms also have stiff "bones" that turn and rotate around simple joints.

MOTOR

CAMERA

GRIPPER

BALL AND SOCKET JOINT

WELDING TORCH

PIVOT JOINT

MORE GRIPPERS

HINGE JOINT

DRILL

Arm muscles move your bones when they receive electrical signals sent along nerves from your brain.

Engineers design robotic arms to be fitted with tools like drills and grippers that pick up and carry things. Sensors can be added to tell how hard the robot is gripping.

MOTOR

Motors in each joint power robotic arm movements and are controlled by electrical signals from a computer "brain."

MOTOR

When a worker trains a robotic arm to do a job, it remembers how.

POWER AND "BRAIN"

8

ALL TOGETHER NOW
In a hive, honeybees work together to clean, tend the young, make food, and guard the nest. Like honeybees, hundreds of small robots can work together to get tasks done.

Swarm robots can do more things working together than each could do on its own. The swarm robots communicate using infrared light waves.

Small robots that join together are called a swarm. A swarm can form shapes, move along a specific path, or follow a leader robot.

Each robot is engineered to move on its legs, powered by battery-run motors.

BATTERY

MOTOR

CONTROL BOARD

INFRARED RECEIVER

INFRARED TRANSMITTER

LEG

9

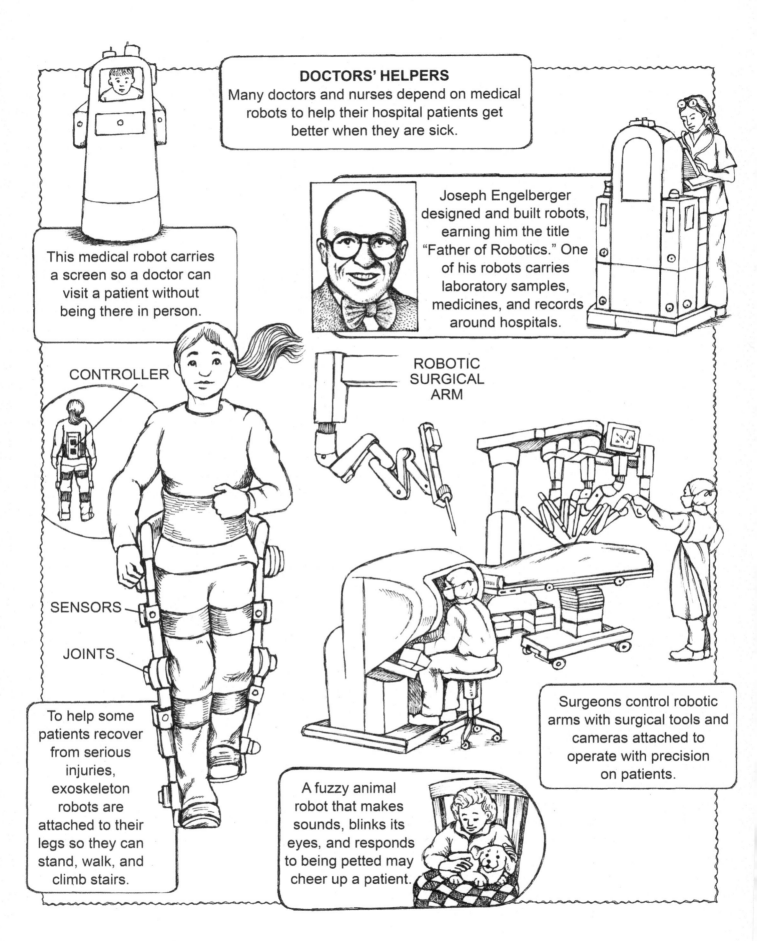

DOCTORS' HELPERS
Many doctors and nurses depend on medical robots to help their hospital patients get better when they are sick.

This medical robot carries a screen so a doctor can visit a patient without being there in person.

Joseph Engelberger designed and built robots, earning him the title "Father of Robotics." One of his robots carries laboratory samples, medicines, and records around hospitals.

CONTROLLER

SENSORS

JOINTS

ROBOTIC SURGICAL ARM

To help some patients recover from serious injuries, exoskeleton robots are attached to their legs so they can stand, walk, and climb stairs.

A fuzzy animal robot that makes sounds, blinks its eyes, and responds to being petted may cheer up a patient.

Surgeons control robotic arms with surgical tools and cameras attached to operate with precision on patients.

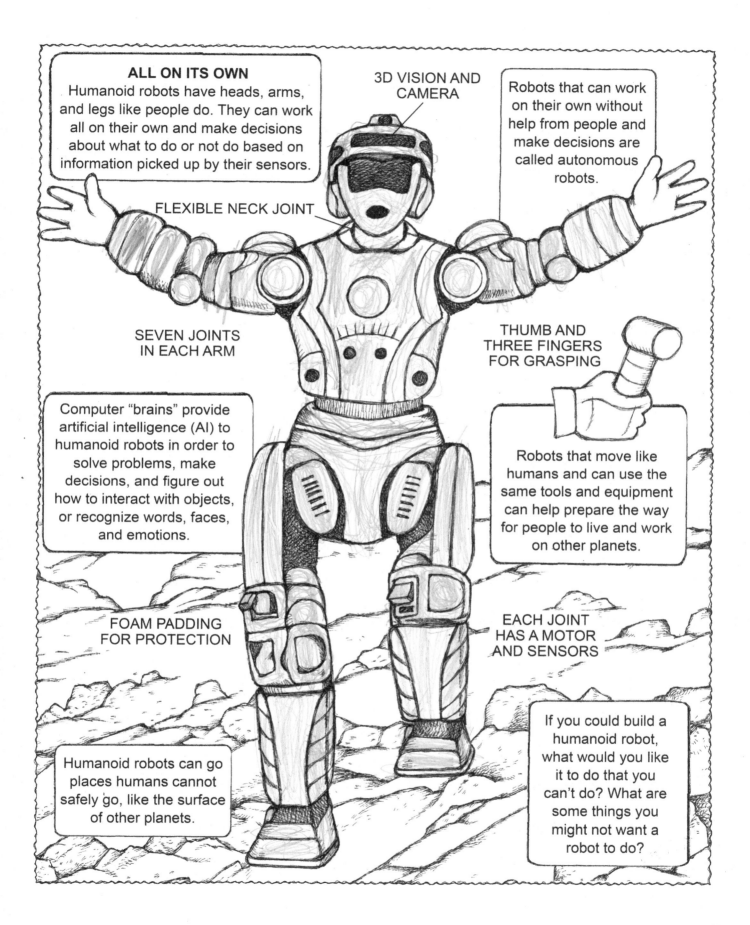

ROBOTS ON MARS
Planets like Mars lack oxygen, making them dangerous for human beings to explore. Robots help prepare the way for future exploration by sending information and images back to Earth.

DEIMOS

PHOBOS

Photos taken by *Curiosity* of the Martian moons Phobos and Deimos were sent back to Earth with images of the Martian landscape.

Robots sent into space are controlled from Earth using high-frequency radio waves.

CURIOSITY

SHERLOC searches for molecules of life, and *WATSON* is a camera.

The *Curiosity* rover robot landed on Mars in 2012 with cameras, wind sensors, radiation detectors, and other equipment.

DRILL

On board *Curiosity* is a nuclear power system that makes electricity and charges the rover's batteries.

The rover's robotic arm collects rocks and soil as it uses lasers to search for chemical signs of past life on Mars.

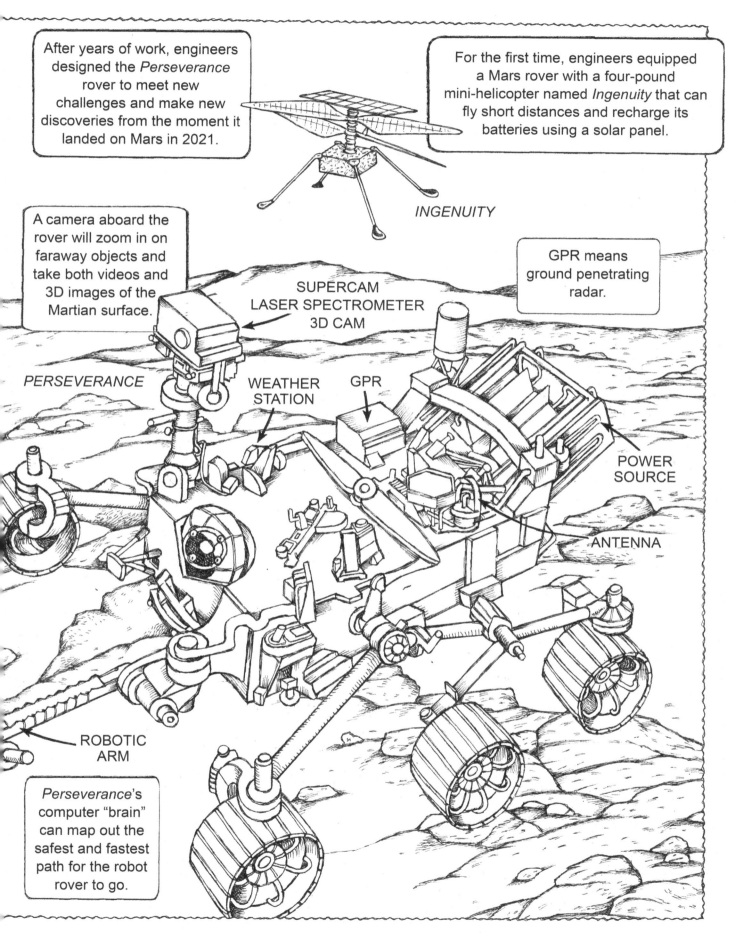

After years of work, engineers designed the *Perseverance* rover to meet new challenges and make new discoveries from the moment it landed on Mars in 2021.

For the first time, engineers equipped a Mars rover with a four-pound mini-helicopter named *Ingenuity* that can fly short distances and recharge its batteries using a solar panel.

INGENUITY

A camera aboard the rover will zoom in on faraway objects and take both videos and 3D images of the Martian surface.

GPR means ground penetrating radar.

SUPERCAM
LASER SPECTROMETER
3D CAM

PERSEVERANCE

WEATHER STATION

GPR

POWER SOURCE

ANTENNA

ROBOTIC ARM

Perseverance's computer "brain" can map out the safest and fastest path for the robot rover to go.

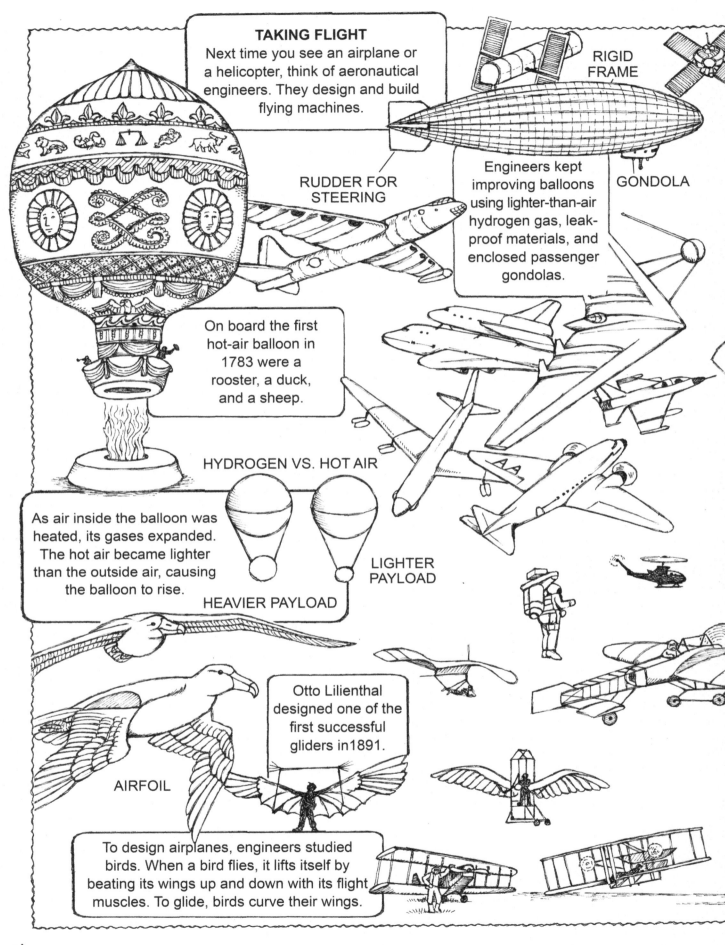

TAKING FLIGHT
Next time you see an airplane or a helicopter, think of aeronautical engineers. They design and build flying machines.

RIGID FRAME

GONDOLA

Engineers kept improving balloons using lighter-than-air hydrogen gas, leak-proof materials, and enclosed passenger gondolas.

RUDDER FOR STEERING

On board the first hot-air balloon in 1783 were a rooster, a duck, and a sheep.

HYDROGEN VS. HOT AIR

As air inside the balloon was heated, its gases expanded. The hot air became lighter than the outside air, causing the balloon to rise.

LIGHTER PAYLOAD

HEAVIER PAYLOAD

AIRFOIL

Otto Lilienthal designed one of the first successful gliders in 1891.

To design airplanes, engineers studied birds. When a bird flies, it lifts itself by beating its wings up and down with its flight muscles. To glide, birds curve their wings.

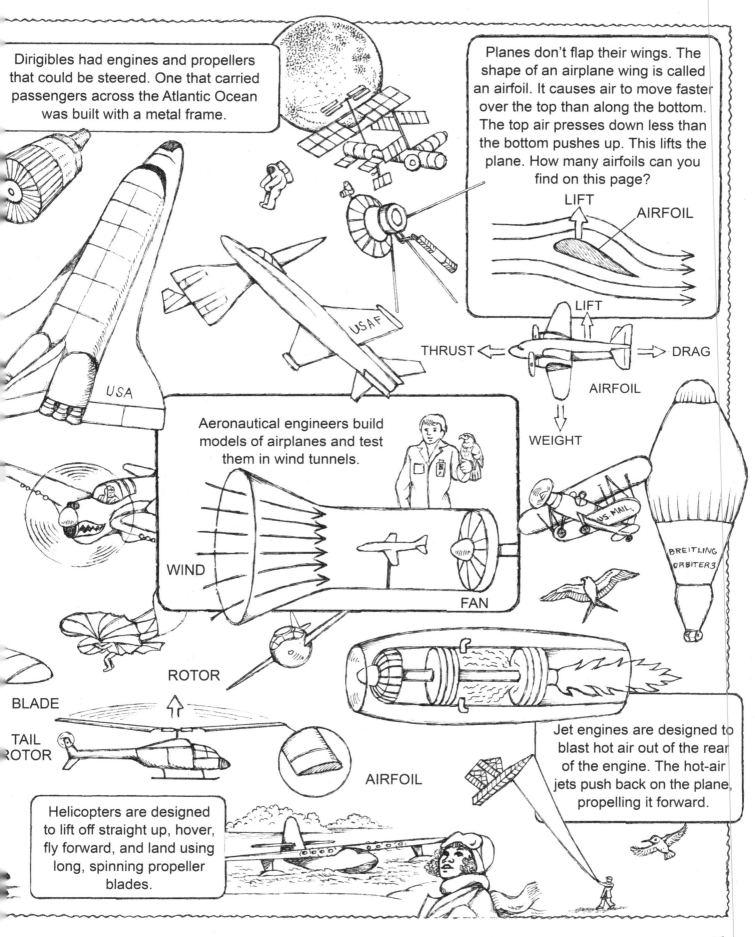

Dirigibles had engines and propellers that could be steered. One that carried passengers across the Atlantic Ocean was built with a metal frame.

Planes don't flap their wings. The shape of an airplane wing is called an airfoil. It causes air to move faster over the top than along the bottom. The top air presses down less than the bottom pushes up. This lifts the plane. How many airfoils can you find on this page?

LIFT

AIRFOIL

LIFT

THRUST

DRAG

AIRFOIL

WEIGHT

USA

USAF

Aeronautical engineers build models of airplanes and test them in wind tunnels.

WIND

FAN

US MAIL

BREITLING ORBITER 3

ROTOR

BLADE

TAIL ROTOR

AIRFOIL

Jet engines are designed to blast hot air out of the rear of the engine. The hot-air jets push back on the plane, propelling it forward.

Helicopters are designed to lift off straight up, hover, fly forward, and land using long, spinning propeller blades.

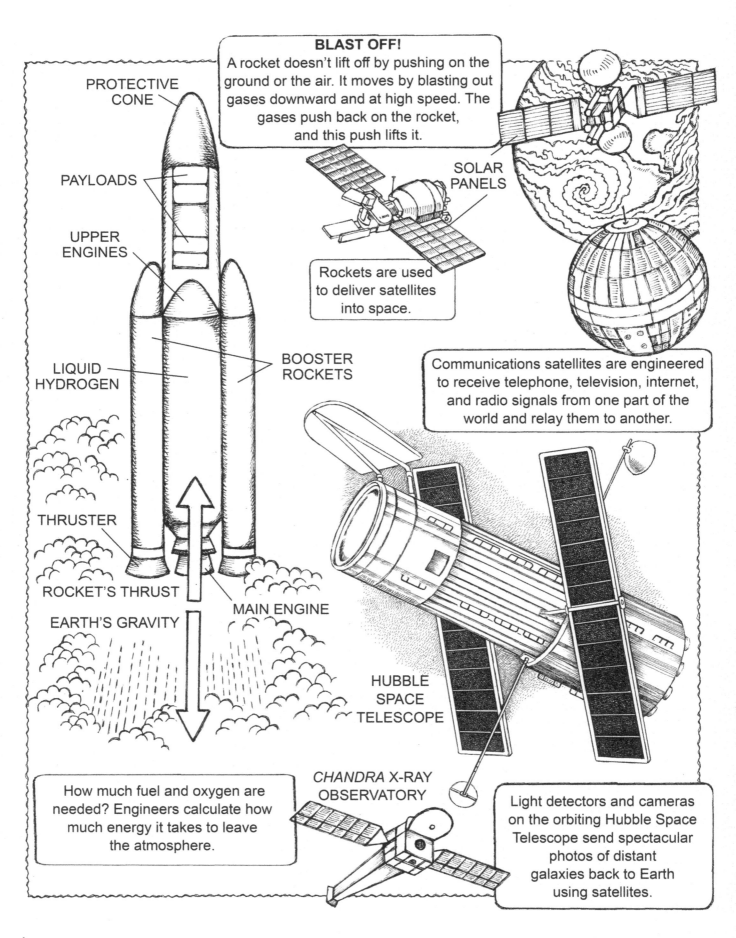

BLAST OFF!
A rocket doesn't lift off by pushing on the ground or the air. It moves by blasting out gases downward and at high speed. The gases push back on the rocket, and this push lifts it.

PROTECTIVE CONE

PAYLOADS

UPPER ENGINES

SOLAR PANELS

Rockets are used to deliver satellites into space.

LIQUID HYDROGEN

BOOSTER ROCKETS

Communications satellites are engineered to receive telephone, television, internet, and radio signals from one part of the world and relay them to another.

THRUSTER

ROCKET'S THRUST

EARTH'S GRAVITY

MAIN ENGINE

HUBBLE SPACE TELESCOPE

How much fuel and oxygen are needed? Engineers calculate how much energy it takes to leave the atmosphere.

CHANDRA X-RAY OBSERVATORY

Light detectors and cameras on the orbiting Hubble Space Telescope send spectacular photos of distant galaxies back to Earth using satellites.

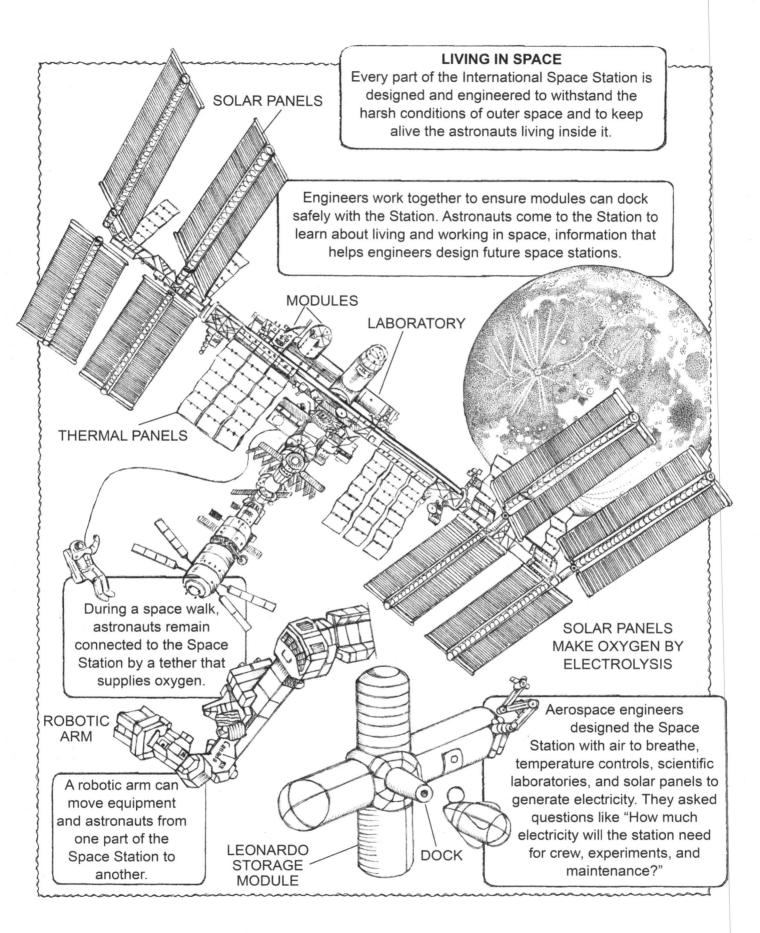

LIVING IN SPACE
Every part of the International Space Station is designed and engineered to withstand the harsh conditions of outer space and to keep alive the astronauts living inside it.

Engineers work together to ensure modules can dock safely with the Station. Astronauts come to the Station to learn about living and working in space, information that helps engineers design future space stations.

SOLAR PANELS

MODULES

LABORATORY

THERMAL PANELS

During a space walk, astronauts remain connected to the Space Station by a tether that supplies oxygen.

SOLAR PANELS MAKE OXYGEN BY ELECTROLYSIS

ROBOTIC ARM

A robotic arm can move equipment and astronauts from one part of the Space Station to another.

LEONARDO STORAGE MODULE

DOCK

Aerospace engineers designed the Space Station with air to breathe, temperature controls, scientific laboratories, and solar panels to generate electricity. They asked questions like "How much electricity will the station need for crew, experiments, and maintenance?"

WORKING WITH ZEROS AND ONES

Computers are everywhere, thanks to engineers who design and redesign their components and programs to make them do more and more tasks faster and faster.

JACQUARD WEAVING
CARD, 1804–05
BASED ON THE BINARY SYSTEM

TRANSISTORS

INACTIVE
CIRCUIT = OFF = 0

ACTIVE
CIRCUIT = ON = 1

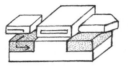

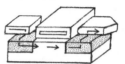

Inside a computer, information is stored using combinations of 0s and 1s to make up binary code. Every letter and number can be translated into binary code.

```
1111000000000101000101
1010001010010010001101
1111000101010000111110
0010110101000110100 10
0100101110001010 11000
0001101011100 10000001
1110101001011100 11001
0101000011110101001 10
0000011101110101010 11
```

A computer only stores zeros and ones, which it keeps track of using an electrical component called a transistor. Like turning on a switch, a 1 in binary code lets electricity flow through a transistor. A 0 stops the flow.

MICROCHIPS

Billions of tiny transistors are needed to make a laptop work. Today those billions of tiny transistors can be combined together on microchips.

These three Black women played a vital role in sending the *Mercury* astronauts into space.

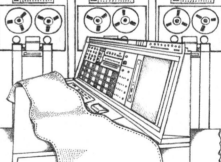

KATHERINE JOHNSON
DOROTHY VAUGHAN
MARY JACKSON

This computer, used at NASA in 1962, had about 50,000 individual transistors to help calculate how to send astronauts into space.

Engineers write programs for computers to help them solve difficult math problems, store vast amounts of information, control robots and other machines, and experiment with designs before they are built.

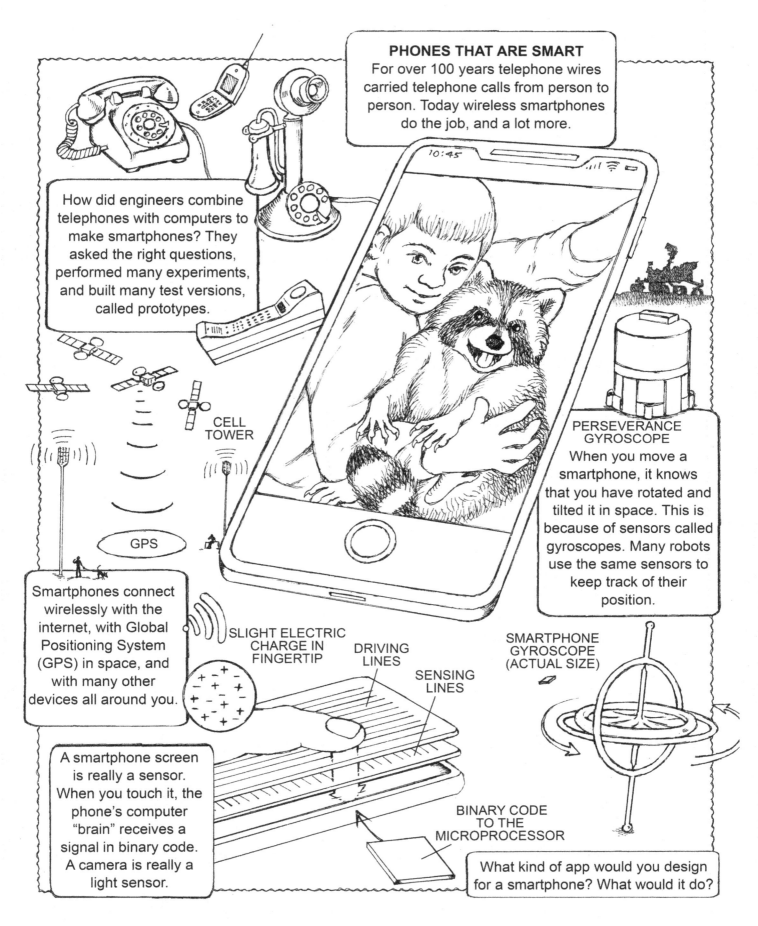

PHONES THAT ARE SMART
For over 100 years telephone wires carried telephone calls from person to person. Today wireless smartphones do the job, and a lot more.

How did engineers combine telephones with computers to make smartphones? They asked the right questions, performed many experiments, and built many test versions, called prototypes.

Smartphones connect wirelessly with the internet, with Global Positioning System (GPS) in space, and with many other devices all around you.

CELL TOWER

GPS

PERSEVERANCE GYROSCOPE
When you move a smartphone, it knows that you have rotated and tilted it in space. This is because of sensors called gyroscopes. Many robots use the same sensors to keep track of their position.

SMARTPHONE GYROSCOPE (ACTUAL SIZE)

SLIGHT ELECTRIC CHARGE IN FINGERTIP

DRIVING LINES

SENSING LINES

A smartphone screen is really a sensor. When you touch it, the phone's computer "brain" receives a signal in binary code. A camera is really a light sensor.

BINARY CODE TO THE MICROPROCESSOR

What kind of app would you design for a smartphone? What would it do?

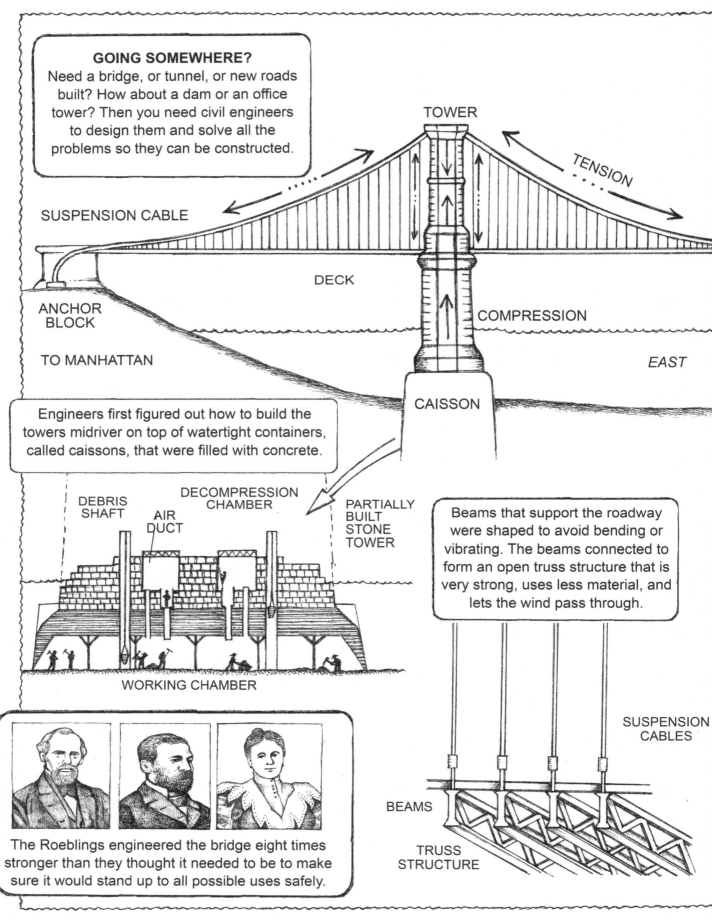

GOING SOMEWHERE?
Need a bridge, or tunnel, or new roads built? How about a dam or an office tower? Then you need civil engineers to design them and solve all the problems so they can be constructed.

SUSPENSION CABLE

TOWER

TENSION

DECK

ANCHOR BLOCK

COMPRESSION

TO MANHATTAN

EAST

CAISSON

Engineers first figured out how to build the towers midriver on top of watertight containers, called caissons, that were filled with concrete.

DEBRIS SHAFT

AIR DUCT

DECOMPRESSION CHAMBER

PARTIALLY BUILT STONE TOWER

Beams that support the roadway were shaped to avoid bending or vibrating. The beams connected to form an open truss structure that is very strong, uses less material, and lets the wind pass through.

WORKING CHAMBER

SUSPENSION CABLES

BEAMS

TRUSS STRUCTURE

The Roeblings engineered the bridge eight times stronger than they thought it needed to be to make sure it would stand up to all possible uses safely.

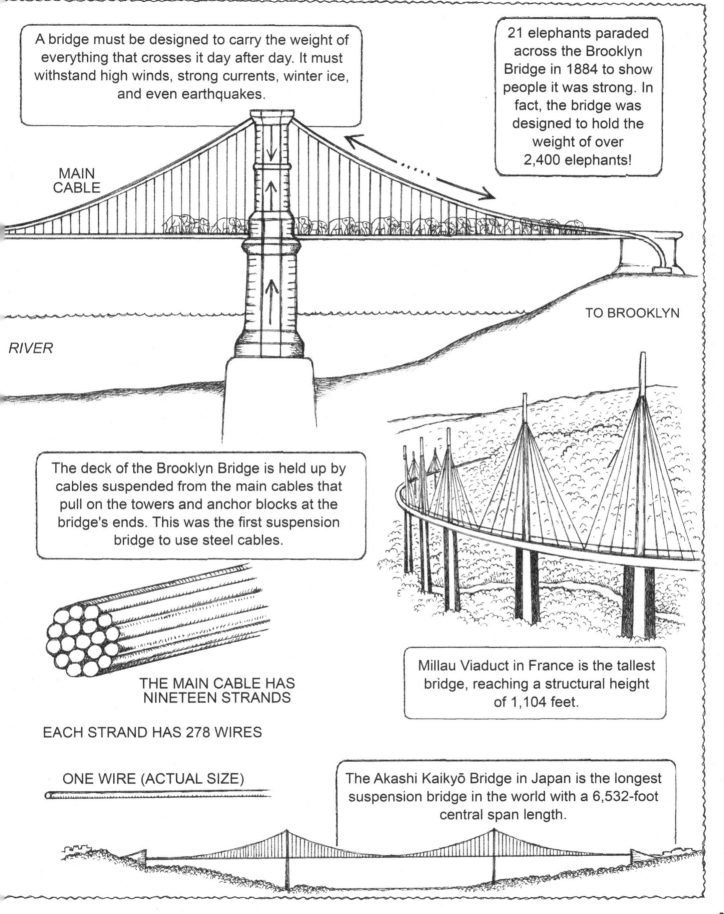

A bridge must be designed to carry the weight of everything that crosses it day after day. It must withstand high winds, strong currents, winter ice, and even earthquakes.

21 elephants paraded across the Brooklyn Bridge in 1884 to show people it was strong. In fact, the bridge was designed to hold the weight of over 2,400 elephants!

MAIN CABLE

TO BROOKLYN

RIVER

The deck of the Brooklyn Bridge is held up by cables suspended from the main cables that pull on the towers and anchor blocks at the bridge's ends. This was the first suspension bridge to use steel cables.

THE MAIN CABLE HAS NINETEEN STRANDS

EACH STRAND HAS 278 WIRES

ONE WIRE (ACTUAL SIZE)

Millau Viaduct in France is the tallest bridge, reaching a structural height of 1,104 feet.

The Akashi Kaikyō Bridge in Japan is the longest suspension bridge in the world with a 6,532-foot central span length.

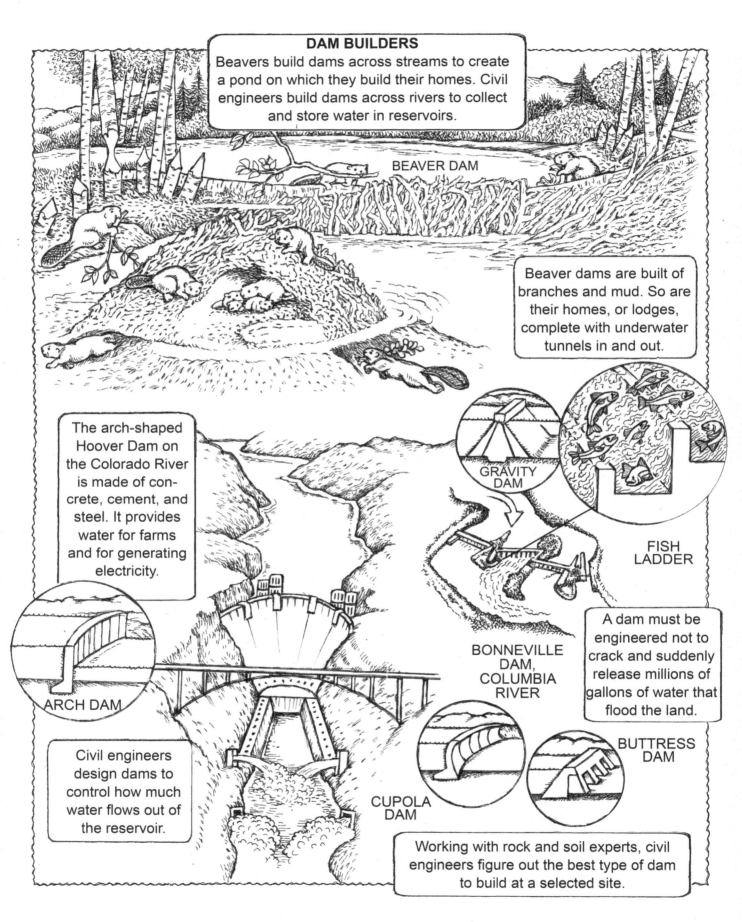

DAM BUILDERS
Beavers build dams across streams to create a pond on which they build their homes. Civil engineers build dams across rivers to collect and store water in reservoirs.

BEAVER DAM

Beaver dams are built of branches and mud. So are their homes, or lodges, complete with underwater tunnels in and out.

GRAVITY DAM

FISH LADDER

The arch-shaped Hoover Dam on the Colorado River is made of concrete, cement, and steel. It provides water for farms and for generating electricity.

BONNEVILLE DAM, COLUMBIA RIVER

A dam must be engineered not to crack and suddenly release millions of gallons of water that flood the land.

ARCH DAM

BUTTRESS DAM

Civil engineers design dams to control how much water flows out of the reservoir.

CUPOLA DAM

Working with rock and soil experts, civil engineers figure out the best type of dam to build at a selected site.

22

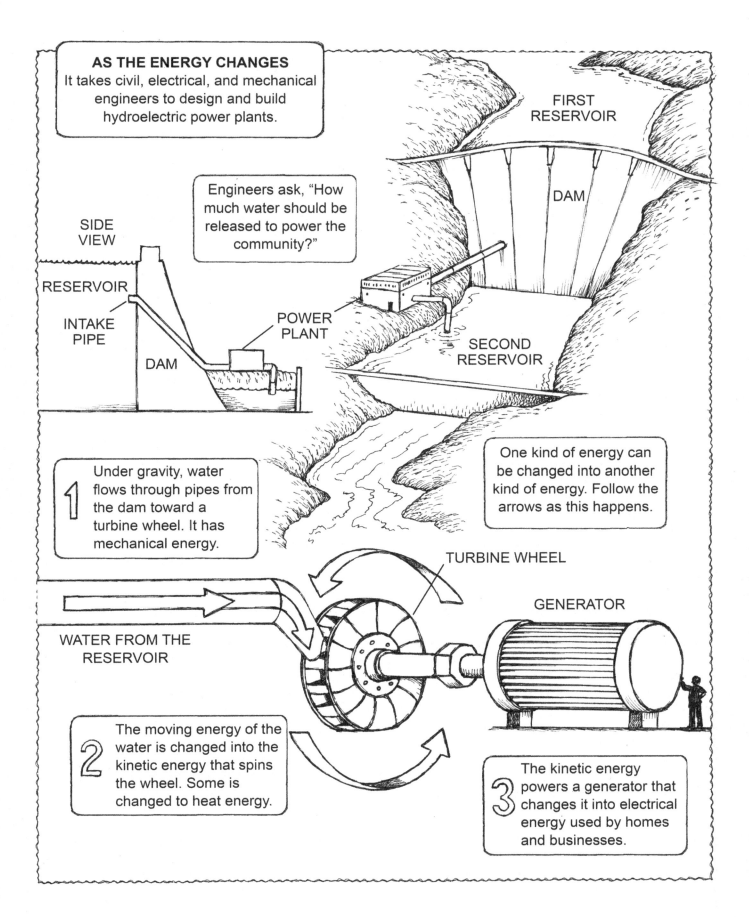

AS THE ENERGY CHANGES
It takes civil, electrical, and mechanical engineers to design and build hydroelectric power plants.

FIRST RESERVOIR

DAM

Engineers ask, "How much water should be released to power the community?"

SIDE VIEW

RESERVOIR

INTAKE PIPE

POWER PLANT

DAM

SECOND RESERVOIR

One kind of energy can be changed into another kind of energy. Follow the arrows as this happens.

1 Under gravity, water flows through pipes from the dam toward a turbine wheel. It has mechanical energy.

TURBINE WHEEL

GENERATOR

WATER FROM THE RESERVOIR

2 The moving energy of the water is changed into the kinetic energy that spins the wheel. Some is changed to heat energy.

3 The kinetic energy powers a generator that changes it into electrical energy used by homes and businesses.

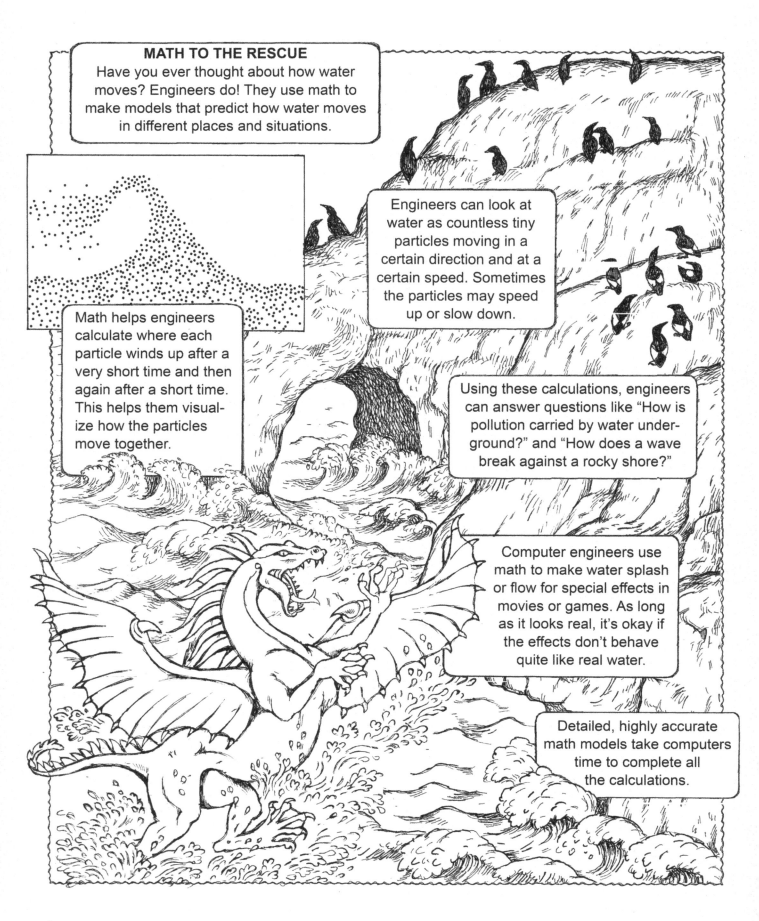

MATH TO THE RESCUE
Have you ever thought about how water moves? Engineers do! They use math to make models that predict how water moves in different places and situations.

Engineers can look at water as countless tiny particles moving in a certain direction and at a certain speed. Sometimes the particles may speed up or slow down.

Math helps engineers calculate where each particle winds up after a very short time and then again after a short time. This helps them visualize how the particles move together.

Using these calculations, engineers can answer questions like "How is pollution carried by water underground?" and "How does a wave break against a rocky shore?"

Computer engineers use math to make water splash or flow for special effects in movies or games. As long as it looks real, it's okay if the effects don't behave quite like real water.

Detailed, highly accurate math models take computers time to complete all the calculations.

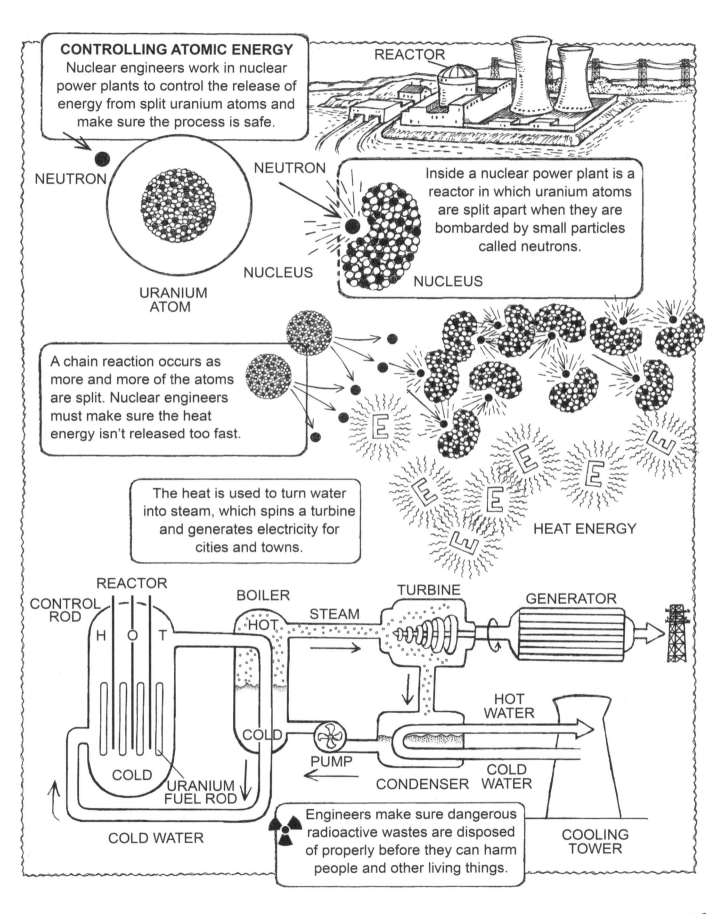

CONTROLLING ATOMIC ENERGY
Nuclear engineers work in nuclear power plants to control the release of energy from split uranium atoms and make sure the process is safe.

REACTOR

NEUTRON

NEUTRON

NUCLEUS

URANIUM ATOM

Inside a nuclear power plant is a reactor in which uranium atoms are split apart when they are bombarded by small particles called neutrons.

NUCLEUS

A chain reaction occurs as more and more of the atoms are split. Nuclear engineers must make sure the heat energy isn't released too fast.

The heat is used to turn water into steam, which spins a turbine and generates electricity for cities and towns.

HEAT ENERGY

CONTROL ROD

REACTOR

BOILER

HOT

STEAM

TURBINE

GENERATOR

H O T

COLD

URANIUM FUEL ROD

COLD

PUMP

CONDENSER

HOT WATER

COLD WATER

COLD WATER

COOLING TOWER

Engineers make sure dangerous radioactive wastes are disposed of properly before they can harm people and other living things.

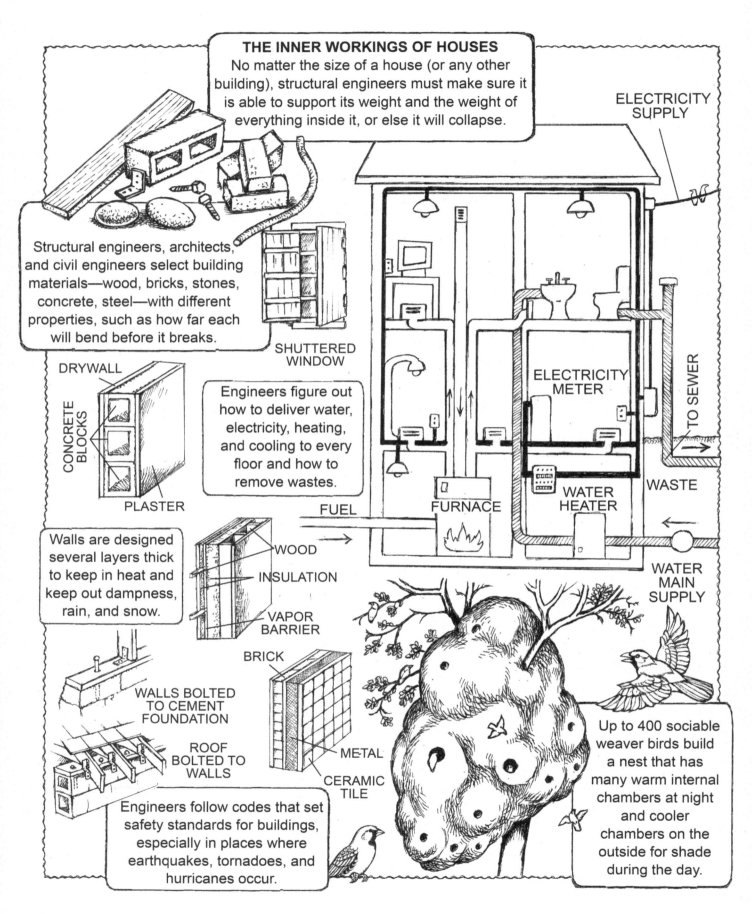

THE INNER WORKINGS OF HOUSES

No matter the size of a house (or any other building), structural engineers must make sure it is able to support its weight and the weight of everything inside it, or else it will collapse.

ELECTRICITY SUPPLY

Structural engineers, architects, and civil engineers select building materials—wood, bricks, stones, concrete, steel—with different properties, such as how far each will bend before it breaks.

SHUTTERED WINDOW

DRYWALL

CONCRETE BLOCKS

PLASTER

ELECTRICITY METER

TO SEWER

Engineers figure out how to deliver water, electricity, heating, and cooling to every floor and how to remove wastes.

FUEL

FURNACE

WATER HEATER

WASTE

WATER MAIN SUPPLY

Walls are designed several layers thick to keep in heat and keep out dampness, rain, and snow.

WOOD

INSULATION

VAPOR BARRIER

BRICK

METAL

CERAMIC TILE

WALLS BOLTED TO CEMENT FOUNDATION

ROOF BOLTED TO WALLS

Engineers follow codes that set safety standards for buildings, especially in places where earthquakes, tornadoes, and hurricanes occur.

Up to 400 sociable weaver birds build a nest that has many warm internal chambers at night and cooler chambers on the outside for shade during the day.

26

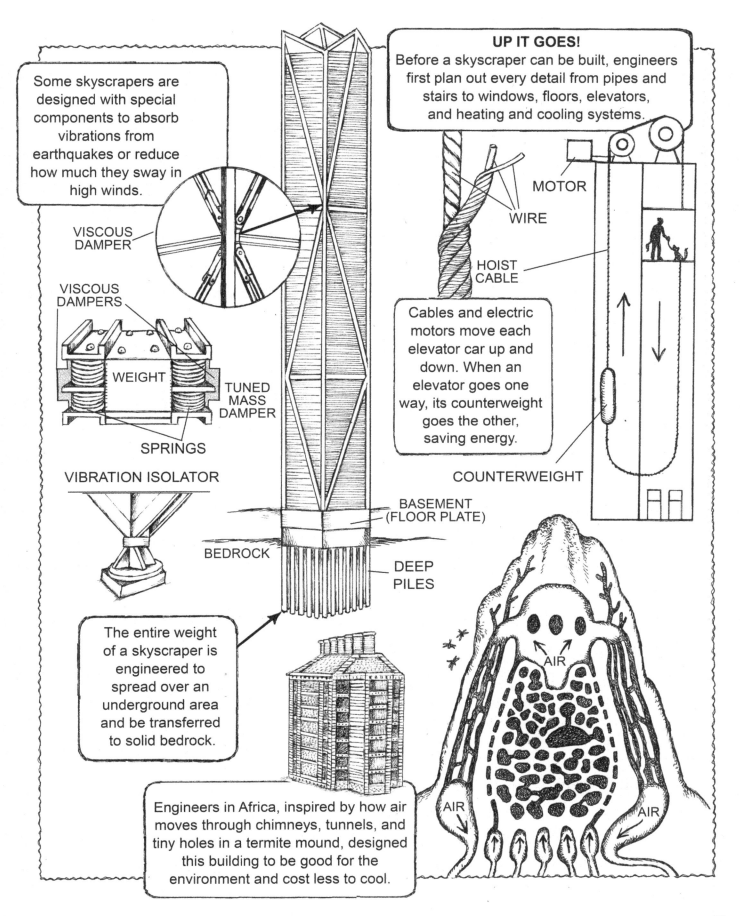

Some skyscrapers are designed with special components to absorb vibrations from earthquakes or reduce how much they sway in high winds.

VISCOUS DAMPER

VISCOUS DAMPERS

WEIGHT

TUNED MASS DAMPER

SPRINGS

VIBRATION ISOLATOR

UP IT GOES!
Before a skyscraper can be built, engineers first plan out every detail from pipes and stairs to windows, floors, elevators, and heating and cooling systems.

MOTOR

WIRE

HOIST CABLE

Cables and electric motors move each elevator car up and down. When an elevator goes one way, its counterweight goes the other, saving energy.

COUNTERWEIGHT

BASEMENT (FLOOR PLATE)

BEDROCK

DEEP PILES

The entire weight of a skyscraper is engineered to spread over an underground area and be transferred to solid bedrock.

Engineers in Africa, inspired by how air moves through chimneys, tunnels, and tiny holes in a termite mound, designed this building to be good for the environment and cost less to cool.

AIR

AIR

AIR

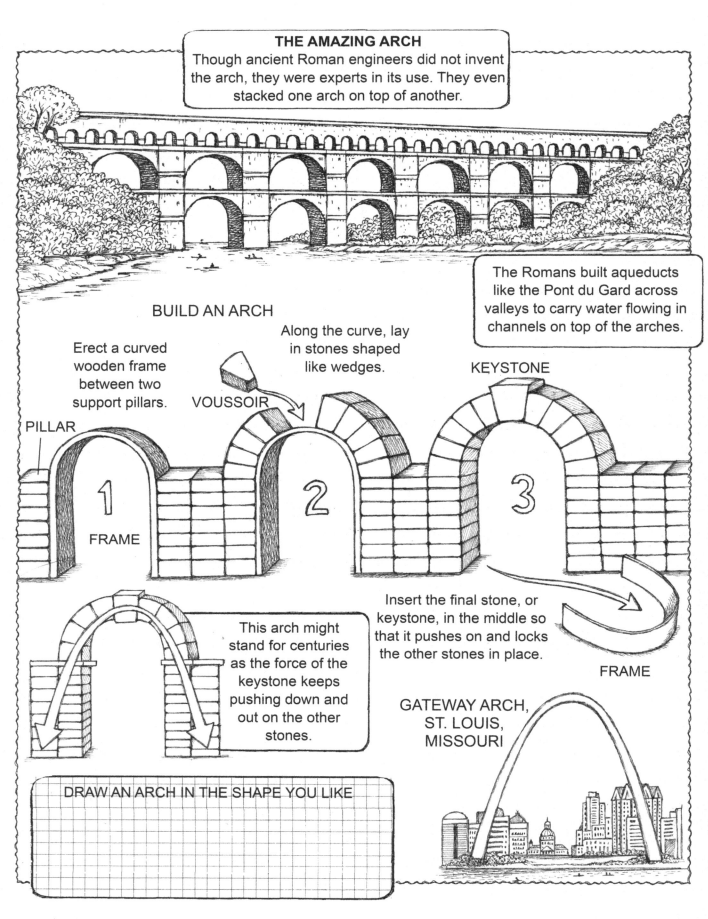

THE AMAZING ARCH
Though ancient Roman engineers did not invent the arch, they were experts in its use. They even stacked one arch on top of another.

The Romans built aqueducts like the Pont du Gard across valleys to carry water flowing in channels on top of the arches.

BUILD AN ARCH

Erect a curved wooden frame between two support pillars.

Along the curve, lay in stones shaped like wedges.

VOUSSOIR

KEYSTONE

PILLAR

1
FRAME

2

3

Insert the final stone, or keystone, in the middle so that it pushes on and locks the other stones in place.

FRAME

This arch might stand for centuries as the force of the keystone keeps pushing down and out on the other stones.

GATEWAY ARCH, ST. LOUIS, MISSOURI

DRAW AN ARCH IN THE SHAPE YOU LIKE

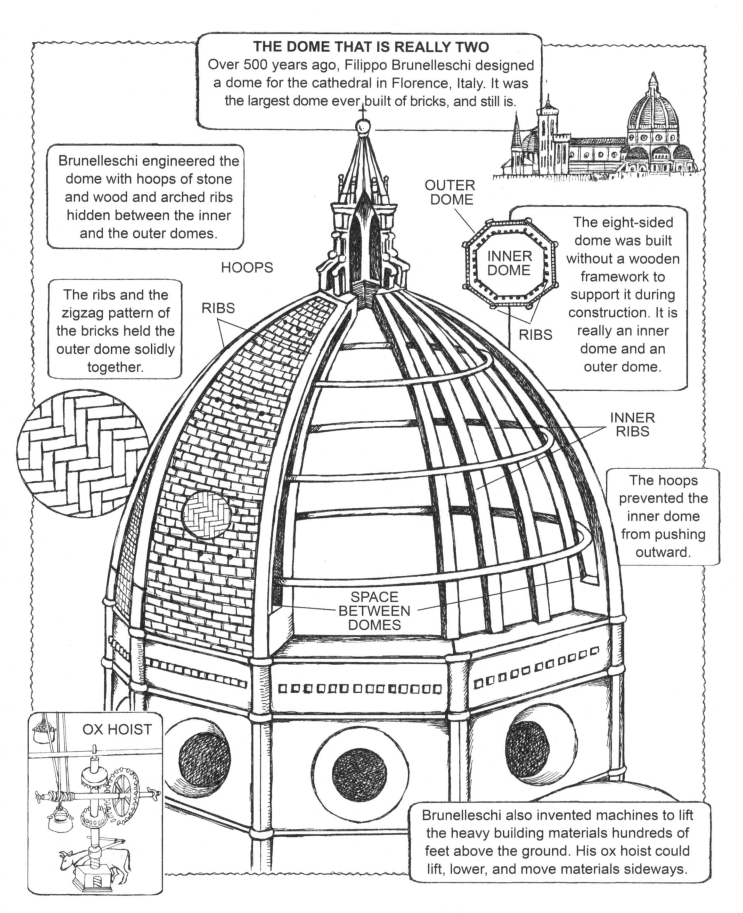

THE DOME THAT IS REALLY TWO
Over 500 years ago, Filippo Brunelleschi designed a dome for the cathedral in Florence, Italy. It was the largest dome ever built of bricks, and still is.

Brunelleschi engineered the dome with hoops of stone and wood and arched ribs hidden between the inner and the outer domes.

HOOPS

The ribs and the zigzag pattern of the bricks held the outer dome solidly together.

RIBS

OUTER DOME

INNER DOME

RIBS

The eight-sided dome was built without a wooden framework to support it during construction. It is really an inner dome and an outer dome.

INNER RIBS

The hoops prevented the inner dome from pushing outward.

SPACE BETWEEN DOMES

OX HOIST

Brunelleschi also invented machines to lift the heavy building materials hundreds of feet above the ground. His ox hoist could lift, lower, and move materials sideways.

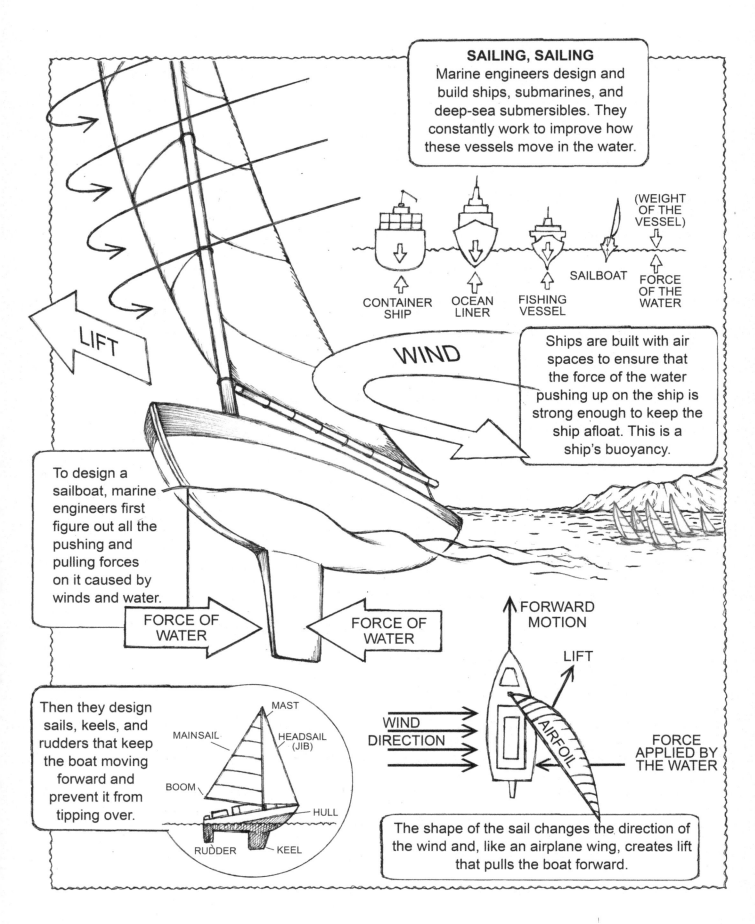

SAILING, SAILING
Marine engineers design and build ships, submarines, and deep-sea submersibles. They constantly work to improve how these vessels move in the water.

(WEIGHT OF THE VESSEL)

FORCE OF THE WATER

CONTAINER SHIP

OCEAN LINER

FISHING VESSEL

SAILBOAT

LIFT

WIND

Ships are built with air spaces to ensure that the force of the water pushing up on the ship is strong enough to keep the ship afloat. This is a ship's buoyancy.

To design a sailboat, marine engineers first figure out all the pushing and pulling forces on it caused by winds and water.

FORCE OF WATER

FORCE OF WATER

FORWARD MOTION

LIFT

WIND DIRECTION

AIRFOIL

FORCE APPLIED BY THE WATER

Then they design sails, keels, and rudders that keep the boat moving forward and prevent it from tipping over.

MAST

MAINSAIL

HEADSAIL (JIB)

BOOM

HULL

RUDDER

KEEL

The shape of the sail changes the direction of the wind and, like an airplane wing, creates lift that pulls the boat forward.

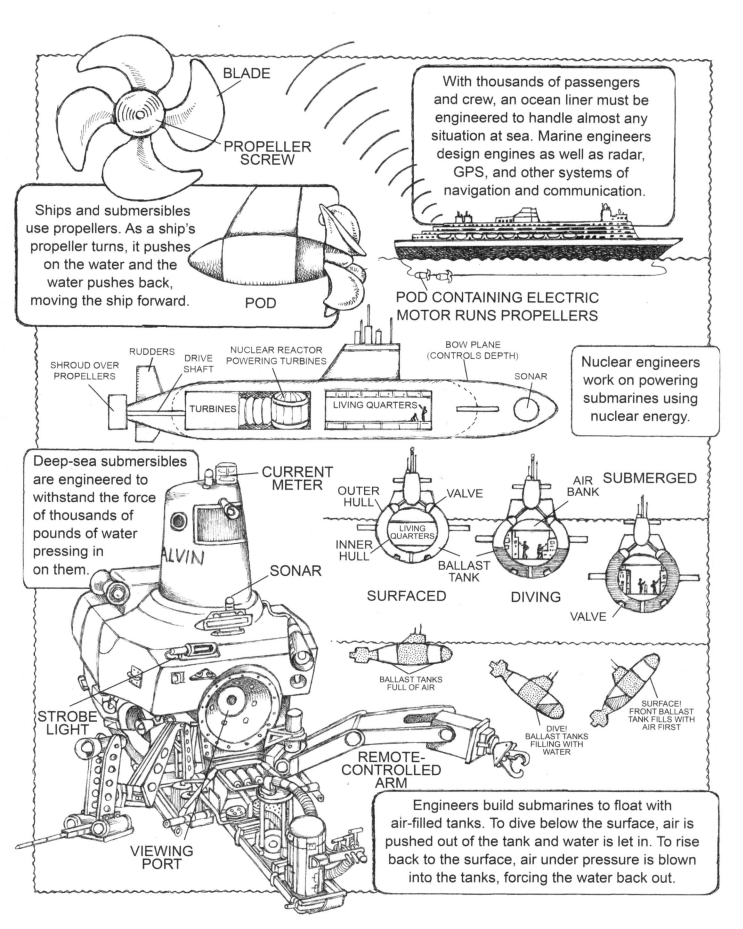

BLADE

PROPELLER SCREW

With thousands of passengers and crew, an ocean liner must be engineered to handle almost any situation at sea. Marine engineers design engines as well as radar, GPS, and other systems of navigation and communication.

Ships and submersibles use propellers. As a ship's propeller turns, it pushes on the water and the water pushes back, moving the ship forward.

POD

POD CONTAINING ELECTRIC MOTOR RUNS PROPELLERS

SHROUD OVER PROPELLERS

RUDDERS

DRIVE SHAFT

NUCLEAR REACTOR POWERING TURBINES

BOW PLANE (CONTROLS DEPTH)

SONAR

TURBINES

LIVING QUARTERS

Nuclear engineers work on powering submarines using nuclear energy.

Deep-sea submersibles are engineered to withstand the force of thousands of pounds of water pressing in on them.

CURRENT METER

OUTER HULL

VALVE

AIR BANK

SUBMERGED

LIVING QUARTERS

INNER HULL

BALLAST TANK

ALVIN

SONAR

SURFACED

DIVING

VALVE

STROBE LIGHT

BALLAST TANKS FULL OF AIR

DIVE! BALLAST TANKS FILLING WITH WATER

SURFACE! FRONT BALLAST TANK FILLS WITH AIR FIRST

REMOTE-CONTROLLED ARM

VIEWING PORT

Engineers build submarines to float with air-filled tanks. To dive below the surface, air is pushed out of the tank and water is let in. To rise back to the surface, air under pressure is blown into the tanks, forcing the water back out.

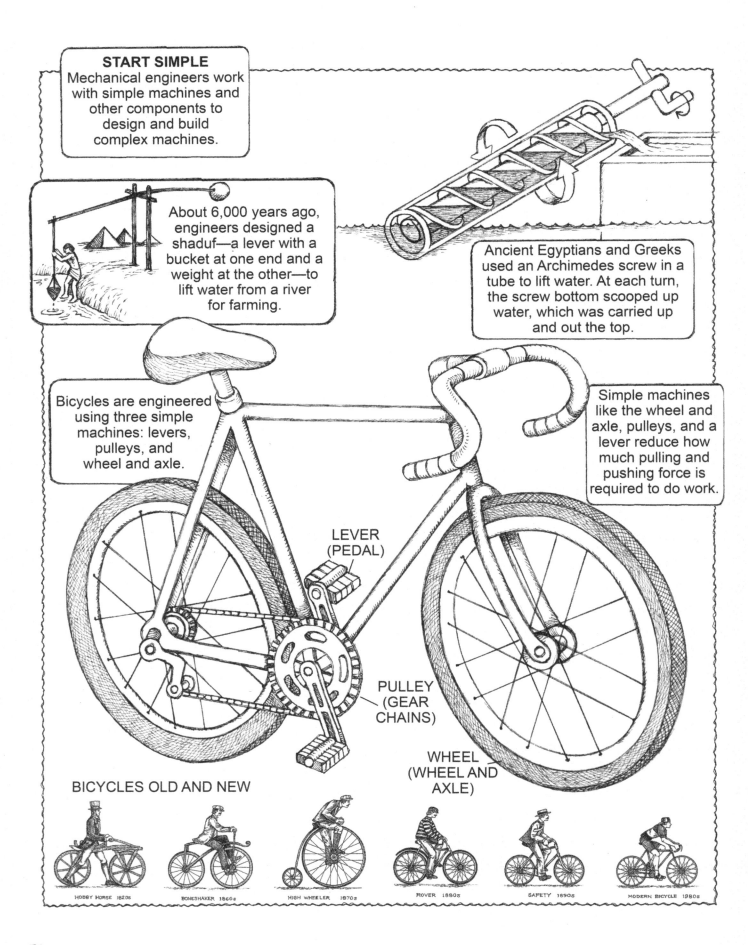

START SIMPLE
Mechanical engineers work with simple machines and other components to design and build complex machines.

About 6,000 years ago, engineers designed a shaduf—a lever with a bucket at one end and a weight at the other—to lift water from a river for farming.

Ancient Egyptians and Greeks used an Archimedes screw in a tube to lift water. At each turn, the screw bottom scooped up water, which was carried up and out the top.

Bicycles are engineered using three simple machines: levers, pulleys, and wheel and axle.

Simple machines like the wheel and axle, pulleys, and a lever reduce how much pulling and pushing force is required to do work.

LEVER (PEDAL)

PULLEY (GEAR CHAINS)

WHEEL (WHEEL AND AXLE)

BICYCLES OLD AND NEW

HOBBY HORSE 1820s

BONESHAKER 1860s

HIGH WHEELER 1870s

ROVER 1880s

SAFETY 1890s

MODERN BICYCLE 1980s

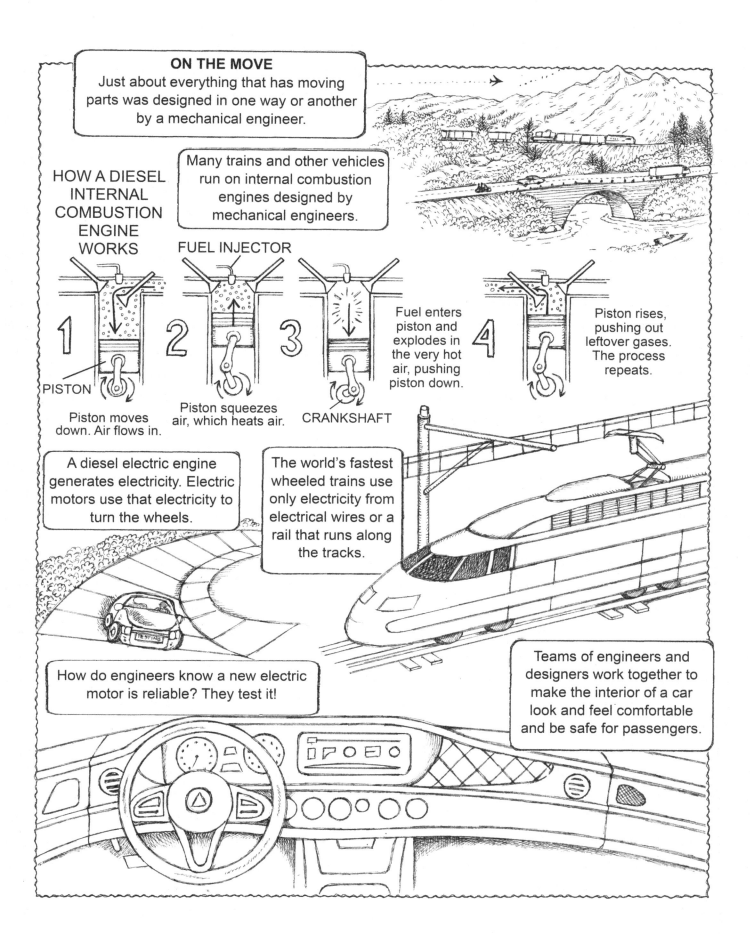

ON THE MOVE
Just about everything that has moving parts was designed in one way or another by a mechanical engineer.

Many trains and other vehicles run on internal combustion engines designed by mechanical engineers.

HOW A DIESEL INTERNAL COMBUSTION ENGINE WORKS

FUEL INJECTOR

1 — PISTON — Piston moves down. Air flows in.

2 — Piston squeezes air, which heats air. CRANKSHAFT

3 — Fuel enters piston and explodes in the very hot air, pushing piston down.

4 — Piston rises, pushing out leftover gases. The process repeats.

A diesel electric engine generates electricity. Electric motors use that electricity to turn the wheels.

The world's fastest wheeled trains use only electricity from electrical wires or a rail that runs along the tracks.

How do engineers know a new electric motor is reliable? They test it!

Teams of engineers and designers work together to make the interior of a car look and feel comfortable and be safe for passengers.

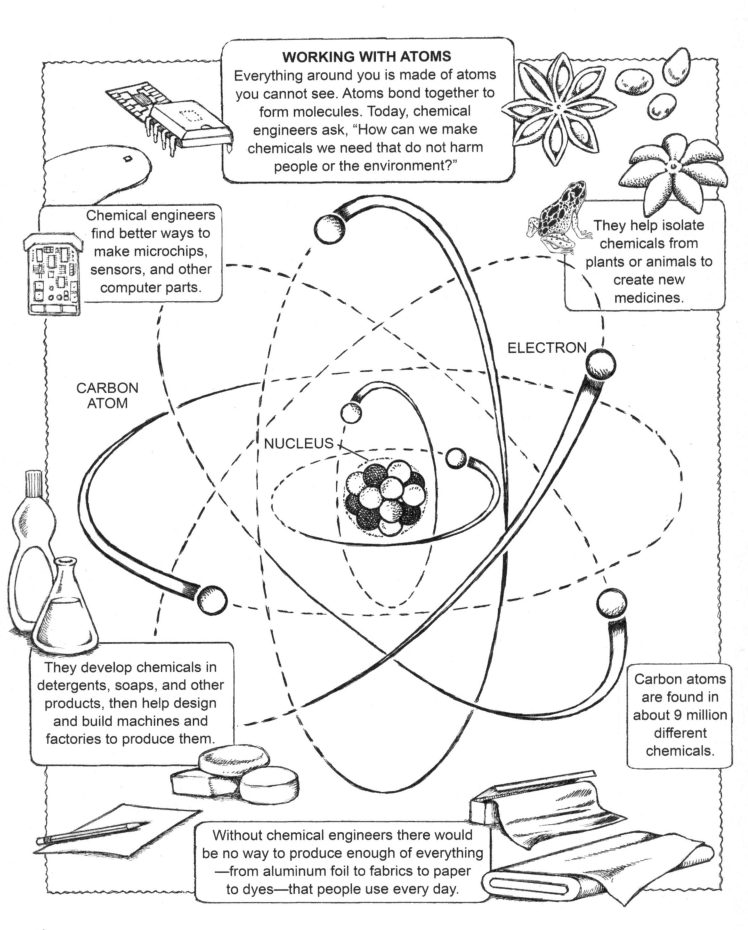

WORKING WITH ATOMS
Everything around you is made of atoms you cannot see. Atoms bond together to form molecules. Today, chemical engineers ask, "How can we make chemicals we need that do not harm people or the environment?"

Chemical engineers find better ways to make microchips, sensors, and other computer parts.

They help isolate chemicals from plants or animals to create new medicines.

ELECTRON

CARBON ATOM

NUCLEUS

They develop chemicals in detergents, soaps, and other products, then help design and build machines and factories to produce them.

Carbon atoms are found in about 9 million different chemicals.

Without chemical engineers there would be no way to produce enough of everything —from aluminum foil to fabrics to paper to dyes—that people use every day.

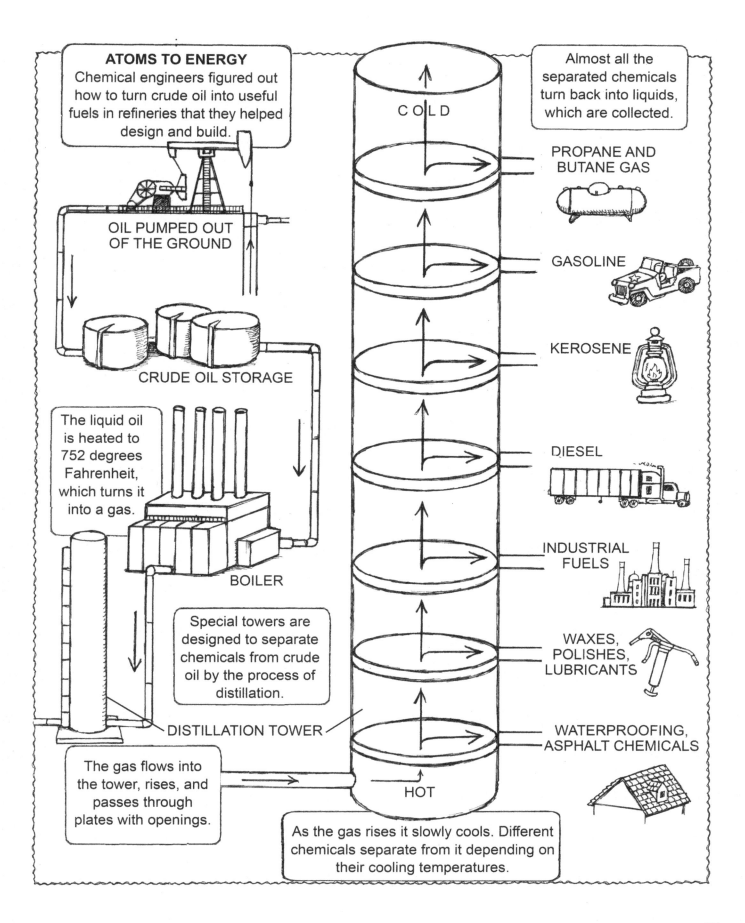

ATOMS TO ENERGY
Chemical engineers figured out how to turn crude oil into useful fuels in refineries that they helped design and build.

OIL PUMPED OUT OF THE GROUND

CRUDE OIL STORAGE

The liquid oil is heated to 752 degrees Fahrenheit, which turns it into a gas.

BOILER

Special towers are designed to separate chemicals from crude oil by the process of distillation.

DISTILLATION TOWER

The gas flows into the tower, rises, and passes through plates with openings.

COLD

HOT

As the gas rises it slowly cools. Different chemicals separate from it depending on their cooling temperatures.

Almost all the separated chemicals turn back into liquids, which are collected.

PROPANE AND BUTANE GAS

GASOLINE

KEROSENE

DIESEL

INDUSTRIAL FUELS

WAXES, POLISHES, LUBRICANTS

WATERPROOFING, ASPHALT CHEMICALS

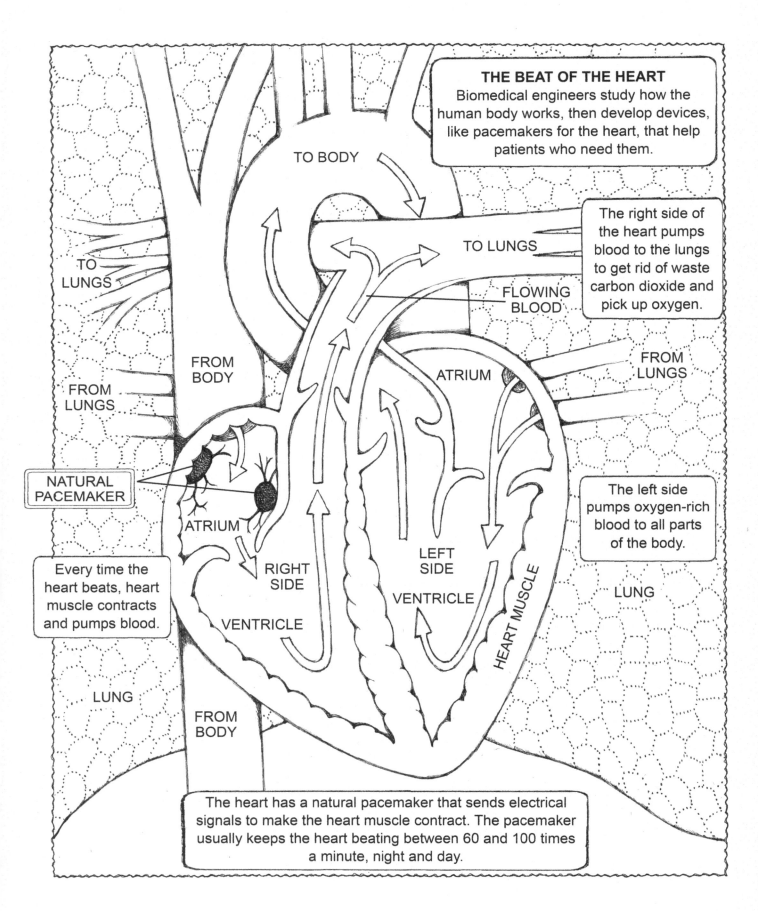

THE BEAT OF THE HEART
Biomedical engineers study how the human body works, then develop devices, like pacemakers for the heart, that help patients who need them.

TO BODY

The right side of the heart pumps blood to the lungs to get rid of waste carbon dioxide and pick up oxygen.

TO LUNGS

TO LUNGS

FLOWING BLOOD

FROM BODY

FROM LUNGS

ATRIUM

FROM LUNGS

NATURAL PACEMAKER

ATRIUM

The left side pumps oxygen-rich blood to all parts of the body.

Every time the heart beats, heart muscle contracts and pumps blood.

RIGHT SIDE

LEFT SIDE

VENTRICLE

HEART MUSCLE

LUNG

VENTRICLE

LUNG

FROM BODY

The heart has a natural pacemaker that sends electrical signals to make the heart muscle contract. The pacemaker usually keeps the heart beating between 60 and 100 times a minute, night and day.

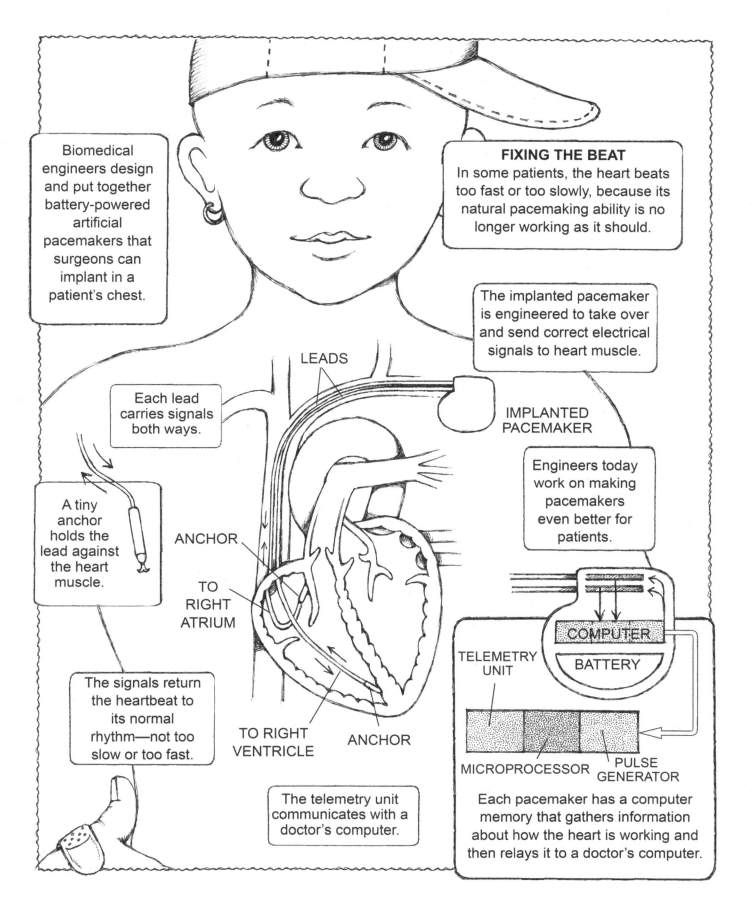

Biomedical engineers design and put together battery-powered artificial pacemakers that surgeons can implant in a patient's chest.

FIXING THE BEAT
In some patients, the heart beats too fast or too slowly, because its natural pacemaking ability is no longer working as it should.

The implanted pacemaker is engineered to take over and send correct electrical signals to heart muscle.

LEADS

Each lead carries signals both ways.

IMPLANTED PACEMAKER

A tiny anchor holds the lead against the heart muscle.

ANCHOR

TO RIGHT ATRIUM

Engineers today work on making pacemakers even better for patients.

COMPUTER

BATTERY

TELEMETRY UNIT

The signals return the heartbeat to its normal rhythm—not too slow or too fast.

TO RIGHT VENTRICLE

ANCHOR

MICROPROCESSOR

PULSE GENERATOR

The telemetry unit communicates with a doctor's computer.

Each pacemaker has a computer memory that gathers information about how the heart is working and then relays it to a doctor's computer.

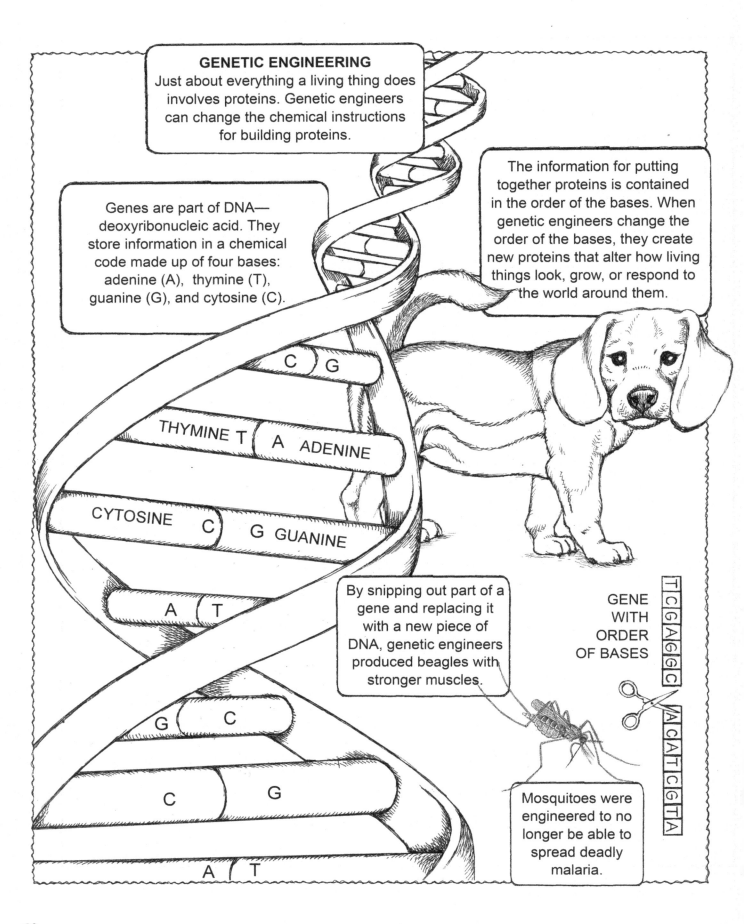

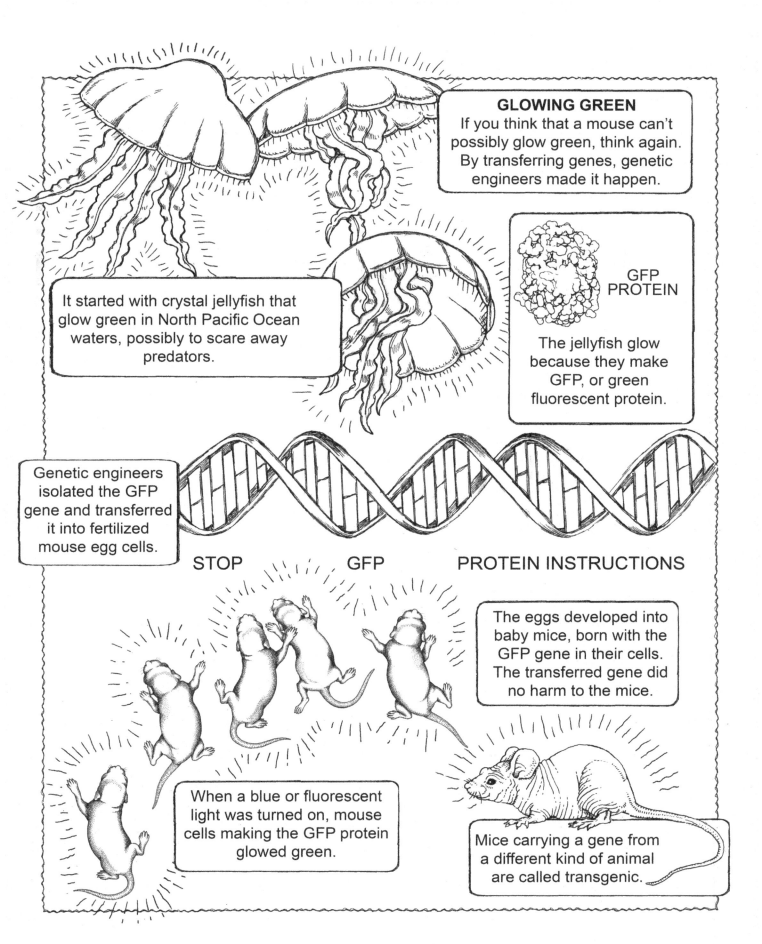

GLOWING GREEN
If you think that a mouse can't possibly glow green, think again. By transferring genes, genetic engineers made it happen.

It started with crystal jellyfish that glow green in North Pacific Ocean waters, possibly to scare away predators.

GFP PROTEIN

The jellyfish glow because they make GFP, or green fluorescent protein.

Genetic engineers isolated the GFP gene and transferred it into fertilized mouse egg cells.

STOP   GFP   PROTEIN INSTRUCTIONS

The eggs developed into baby mice, born with the GFP gene in their cells. The transferred gene did no harm to the mice.

When a blue or fluorescent light was turned on, mouse cells making the GFP protein glowed green.

Mice carrying a gene from a different kind of animal are called transgenic.

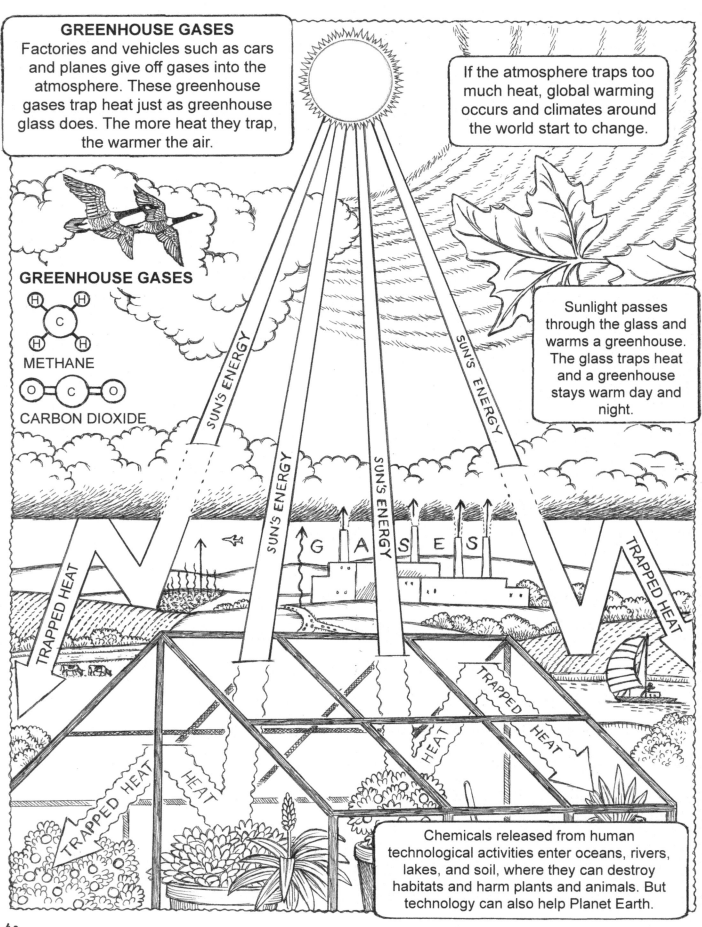

GREENHOUSE GASES
Factories and vehicles such as cars and planes give off gases into the atmosphere. These greenhouse gases trap heat just as greenhouse glass does. The more heat they trap, the warmer the air.

GREENHOUSE GASES

METHANE

CARBON DIOXIDE

If the atmosphere traps too much heat, global warming occurs and climates around the world start to change.

Sunlight passes through the glass and warms a greenhouse. The glass traps heat and a greenhouse stays warm day and night.

Chemicals released from human technological activities enter oceans, rivers, lakes, and soil, where they can destroy habitats and harm plants and animals. But technology can also help Planet Earth.

SUN'S ENERGY

GASES

TRAPPED HEAT

HEAT

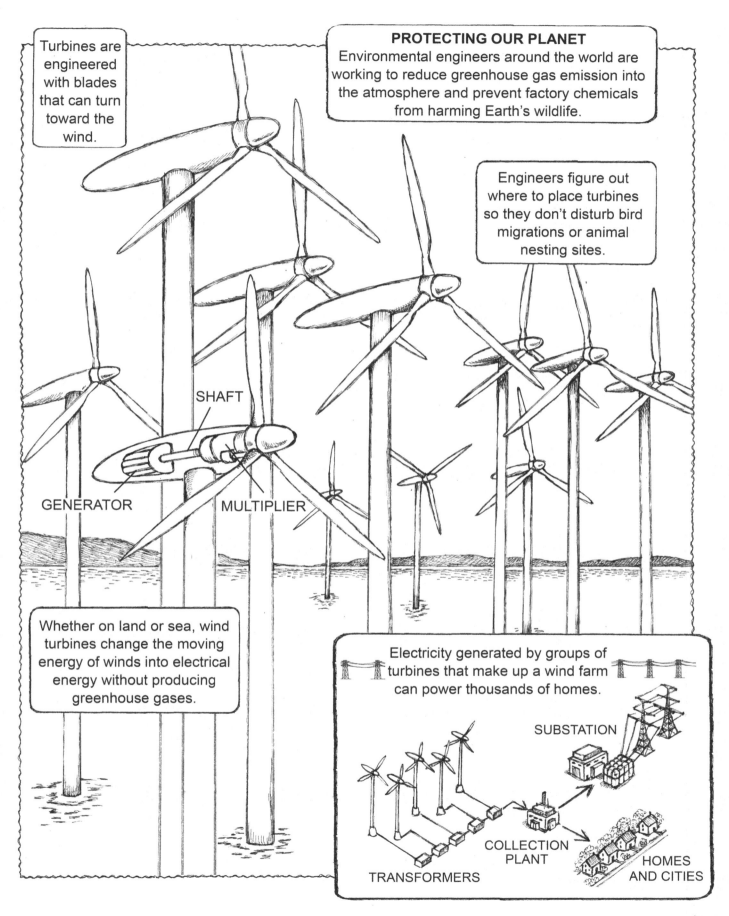

Turbines are engineered with blades that can turn toward the wind.

PROTECTING OUR PLANET
Environmental engineers around the world are working to reduce greenhouse gas emission into the atmosphere and prevent factory chemicals from harming Earth's wildlife.

Engineers figure out where to place turbines so they don't disturb bird migrations or animal nesting sites.

SHAFT

GENERATOR

MULTIPLIER

Whether on land or sea, wind turbines change the moving energy of winds into electrical energy without producing greenhouse gases.

Electricity generated by groups of turbines that make up a wind farm can power thousands of homes.

SUBSTATION

COLLECTION PLANT

TRANSFORMERS

HOMES AND CITIES

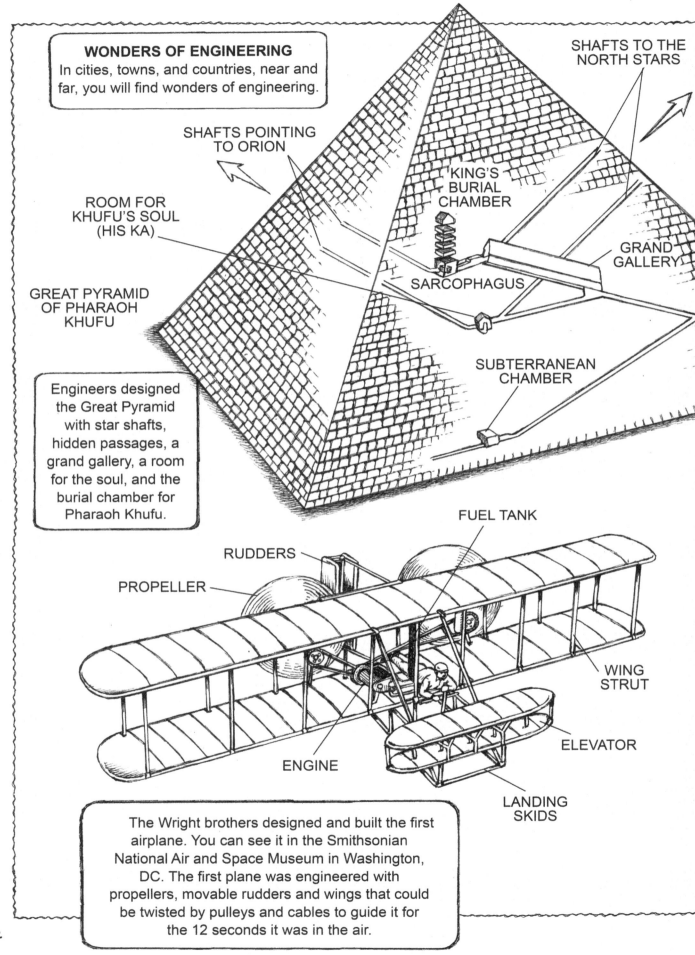

WONDERS OF ENGINEERING
In cities, towns, and countries, near and far, you will find wonders of engineering.

SHAFTS TO THE NORTH STARS

SHAFTS POINTING TO ORION

KING'S BURIAL CHAMBER

ROOM FOR KHUFU'S SOUL (HIS KA)

GRAND GALLERY

SARCOPHAGUS

GREAT PYRAMID OF PHARAOH KHUFU

SUBTERRANEAN CHAMBER

Engineers designed the Great Pyramid with star shafts, hidden passages, a grand gallery, a room for the soul, and the burial chamber for Pharaoh Khufu.

FUEL TANK

RUDDERS

PROPELLER

WING STRUT

ELEVATOR

ENGINE

LANDING SKIDS

The Wright brothers designed and built the first airplane. You can see it in the Smithsonian National Air and Space Museum in Washington, DC. The first plane was engineered with propellers, movable rudders and wings that could be twisted by pulleys and cables to guide it for the 12 seconds it was in the air.

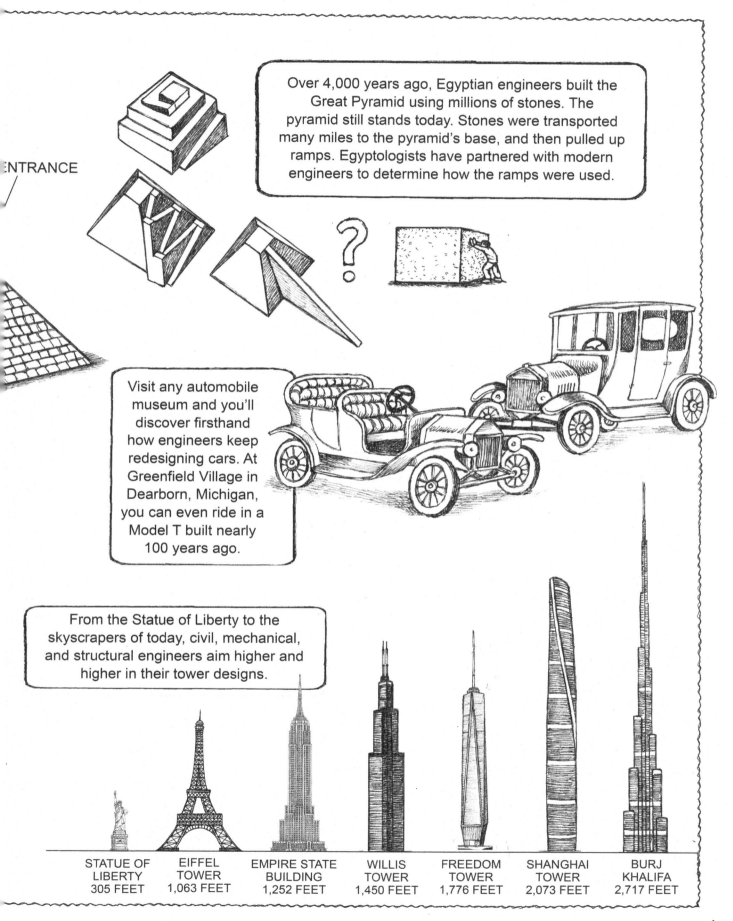

ENTRANCE

Over 4,000 years ago, Egyptian engineers built the Great Pyramid using millions of stones. The pyramid still stands today. Stones were transported many miles to the pyramid's base, and then pulled up ramps. Egyptologists have partnered with modern engineers to determine how the ramps were used.

Visit any automobile museum and you'll discover firsthand how engineers keep redesigning cars. At Greenfield Village in Dearborn, Michigan, you can even ride in a Model T built nearly 100 years ago.

From the Statue of Liberty to the skyscrapers of today, civil, mechanical, and structural engineers aim higher and higher in their tower designs.

STATUE OF LIBERTY
305 FEET

EIFFEL TOWER
1,063 FEET

EMPIRE STATE BUILDING
1,252 FEET

WILLIS TOWER
1,450 FEET

FREEDOM TOWER
1,776 FEET

SHANGHAI TOWER
2,073 FEET

BURJ KHALIFA
2,717 FEET

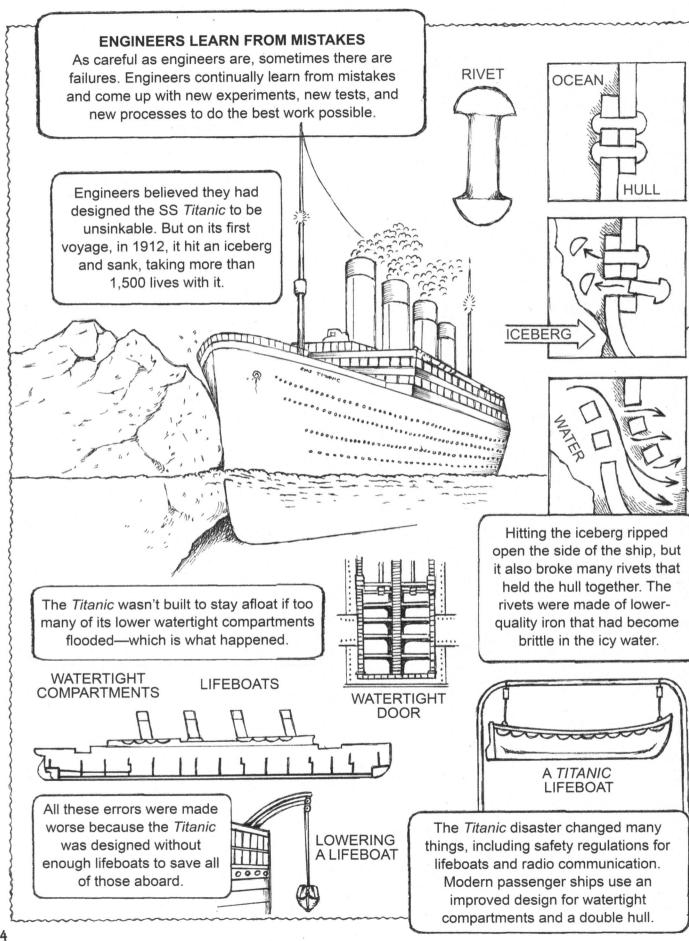

ENGINEERS LEARN FROM MISTAKES
As careful as engineers are, sometimes there are failures. Engineers continually learn from mistakes and come up with new experiments, new tests, and new processes to do the best work possible.

Engineers believed they had designed the SS *Titanic* to be unsinkable. But on its first voyage, in 1912, it hit an iceberg and sank, taking more than 1,500 lives with it.

RIVET

OCEAN

HULL

ICEBERG

WATER

Hitting the iceberg ripped open the side of the ship, but it also broke many rivets that held the hull together. The rivets were made of lower-quality iron that had become brittle in the icy water.

The *Titanic* wasn't built to stay afloat if too many of its lower watertight compartments flooded—which is what happened.

WATERTIGHT COMPARTMENTS

LIFEBOATS

WATERTIGHT DOOR

A *TITANIC* LIFEBOAT

All these errors were made worse because the *Titanic* was designed without enough lifeboats to save all of those aboard.

LOWERING A LIFEBOAT

The *Titanic* disaster changed many things, including safety regulations for lifeboats and radio communication. Modern passenger ships use an improved design for watertight compartments and a double hull.

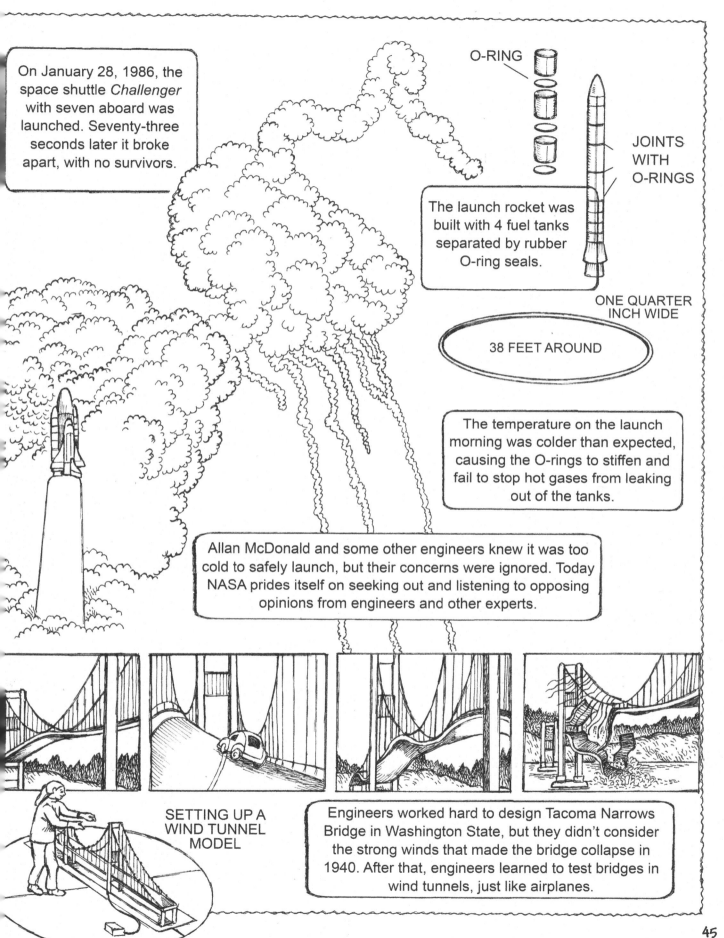

On January 28, 1986, the space shuttle *Challenger* with seven aboard was launched. Seventy-three seconds later it broke apart, with no survivors.

O-RING

JOINTS WITH O-RINGS

The launch rocket was built with 4 fuel tanks separated by rubber O-ring seals.

ONE QUARTER INCH WIDE

38 FEET AROUND

The temperature on the launch morning was colder than expected, causing the O-rings to stiffen and fail to stop hot gases from leaking out of the tanks.

Allan McDonald and some other engineers knew it was too cold to safely launch, but their concerns were ignored. Today NASA prides itself on seeking out and listening to opposing opinions from engineers and other experts.

SETTING UP A WIND TUNNEL MODEL

Engineers worked hard to design Tacoma Narrows Bridge in Washington State, but they didn't consider the strong winds that made the bridge collapse in 1940. After that, engineers learned to test bridges in wind tunnels, just like airplanes.

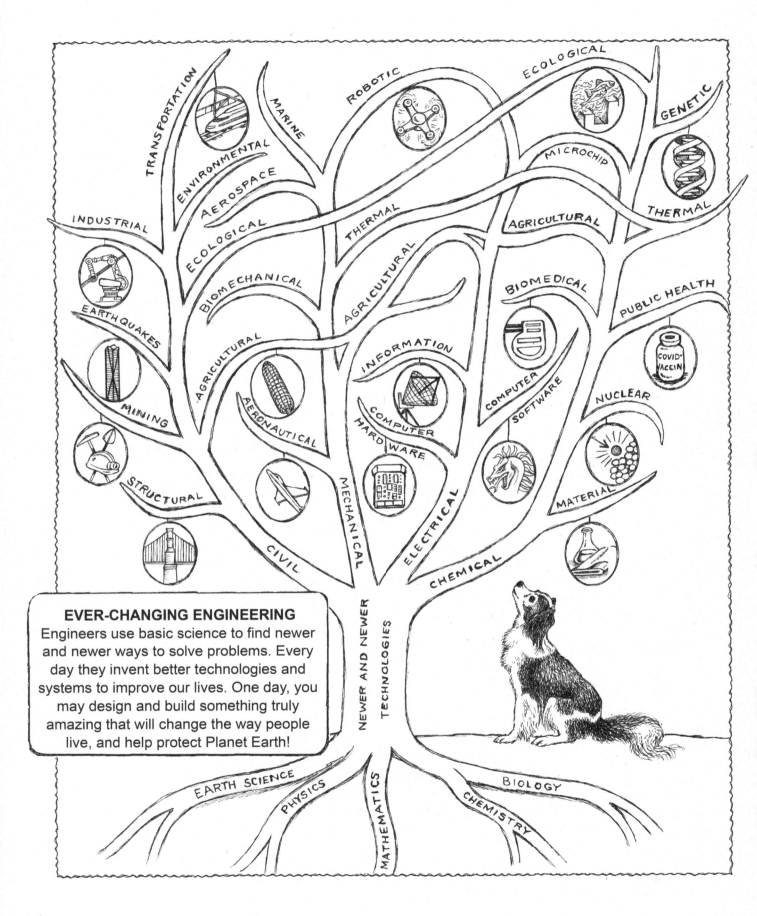

EVER-CHANGING ENGINEERING
Engineers use basic science to find newer and newer ways to solve problems. Every day they invent better technologies and systems to improve our lives. One day, you may design and build something truly amazing that will change the way people live, and help protect Planet Earth!